The Italian Cookbook for Beginners

Over 100 Classic Recipes with Everyday Ingredients

The Italian Cookbook for Beginners

SALINAS PRESS

Contents

Introduction

Believe it or not, there's no such thing as Italian food. In fact, the cuisine of Italy is a mosaic of regional cuisines unique to areas such as Bologna, Milan, Naples, Piedmont, Rome, Sicily, Tuscany, and Venice. For centuries, Italy's boot and islands were divided into more than a dozen separate kingdoms, republics, and duchies with their own laws, languages, cultures . . . and cooking traditions.

It wasn't until 1861 that the Italian Peninsula's numerous states were unified into a single nation, but even now, the food of Italy encompasses the dishes of nearly twenty different, distinctive, regional cuisines. The eggplant, citrus, swordfish, and anchovy dishes of Sicily so influenced by Spanish, Greek, and Arabic flavors have little in common with the Austrian-, Hungarian-, and Croatian-influenced stews and cured meats of Friuli-Venezia Giulia.

Then there's the New World. Many of the ingredients now central in Italian cookery—tomatoes, bell peppers, zucchini, beans, cornmeal, and others—didn't even exist in Europe until the explorers of the sixteenth, seventeenth, and eighteenth centuries imported them from North and South America. And ever since Italian immigrants began to arrive in the United States in the nineteenth century, they've created an entirely new cuisine: Italian American. Meatball heroes, chicken parmigiana, and baked ziti are as purely American as pot roast, po' boys, and peanut butter. Dishes that originated in Italy, such as pizza and lasagna, have been given such a powerful American twist that they're in a culinary category all their own.

Put it all together, though, and the result is a vibrant mélange of fresh, robust flavors; rich, enticing aromas; intriguing, complementary textures; and gorgeous, exuberant colors. It all melds together into one of America's favorite cuisines. In all its variety, Italian-inflected cookery draws almost everyone to the table and almost every amateur chef to the kitchen. Yet, this delicious food is surprisingly easy to make! You don't need fancy techniques, hard-to-find ingredients, or specialized tools to create mouthwatering Italian dishes; all you need is a desire to *mangia*.

Read on and you'll find everything you need to know about cooking Italian for yourself, your family, and your friends. *Buon appetito!*

How to Eat Italian

Italians traditionally considered *pranzo* (lunch) the main meal of the day. In the afternoons, workplaces and schools would shut down for a few hours, and workers and children would return home to eat. Dining was leisurely and sumptuous, with several courses eaten in succession. Times have changed, though, as the pace of business and the number of working women has rapidly increased. But most shops still shut down from about 1:00 or 1:30 p.m. to 3:30 or 4:00 p.m. for *pausa pranzo* (lunch break), a throwback to the old days. Today the bounteous meal that once was lunch in Italy has shifted to the evening hours.

A full-on *cena* (dinner) can consist of as many as seven courses: *aperitivo* (hors d'oeuvres), *antipasto* (appetizer), *primo* (first course, usually pasta), *secondo* with *contorno* (second course, usually fish, poultry, or meat, with vegetables), *insalata* (salad), *formaggi e frutta* (cheese and fruit), and *dolce* (dessert). For the most part, though, the everyday meal in Italy has two or three courses: *primo, secondo* with *contorno*, and possibly *dolce*. Unless you're entertaining guests, you're more likely to eat one, two, or three courses at dinner, perhaps an antipasto or insalata, a main course—either a pasta or a protein with sides—and dessert. Your salad will come before instead of after the main course; you're unlikely to eat both a pasta dish and a meat dish at the same meal; and you don't think of cheese and fruit as a follow-up to an entrée.

It's easy to plug Italian dishes into an American meal plan. As with any dinner, it's just a matter of balancing flavors, aligning heartiness, and accounting for nutrition. When you put together a menu the Italian way, harmonizing the courses is considered just as important as balancing the ingredients in a dish. Likewise, when you design a meal that includes lots of courses or multiple dishes per course, follow Italian tradition by planning on smaller servings. Here are a few examples of the kinds of dinner menus you might build from the recipes in this book:

LIGHT WEEKNIGHT MENU

Insalata Caprese
Salmon with Lemon, Capers, and Rosemary
Sautéed Greens
Affogato

BIG WEEKNIGHT MENU

Minestrone
Chicken Cacciatore
Cauliflower Gratin
Roasted Potatoes
Olive Oil Cake

FESTIVE WEEKEND MENU

Panfried Calamari
Pizza Marinara with Toppings
Stuffed Artichokes
Lemon-Ricotta Cookies

FAMILY HOLIDAY MENU

Traditional Antipasto Platter
Garlic Bread
Lasagna
Roasted Balsamic Chicken
Zucchini Ripieni
Ricotta Cheesecake

DINNER PARTY MENU

Tomato and Basil Bruschetta
Stuffed Mushrooms
Insalata Tricolore
Butternut Squash or Pumpkin Ravioli with Sage and Brown Butter–Sauce
Veal Piccata
Lemon-Ricotta Cookies
Tiramisu

Olive Oil

As you'll see from recipe to recipe and chapter to chapter, *olio di olivia* (olive oil) is the almost universal ingredient in Italian cooking, even appearing in some desserts. Its beautiful flavors are all the more appealing when you remember the health benefits that olive oil offers. But even if it were bad for your health, your taste buds would still find it very, very good. Using the right olive oil for each recipe is key to making every dish the very best it can be. Don't panic! You don't need to run out and buy half a dozen varieties of olive oil—unless you want to, of course. All you need is a good-quality cooking oil and a good finishing oil. Where to start?

You'll find several types of olive oil on your supermarket shelf:

- ***Extra-Virgin Olive Oil (EVOO):*** This is what it's all about. The highest grade of olive oil, EVOO is the most flavorful of all. The term *virgin* refers to the first pressing of the fruit (yes, olives are a fruit), which yields the freshest-flavored juice. Oils labeled "extra-virgin" are made using a method called cold pressing, which involves no chemical treatment and so produces the purest kind of olive oil. It's also the most expensive, but it really does deliver the best results in the kitchen, so it's entirely worth a couple more dollars.

    Good EVOOs have a fruity flavor along with varying degrees of pepperiness, and range in color from pale gold, which generally indicates a milder flavor, to bright green, which typically signifies more intensity. If it's cloudy, it's generally even more complex in flavor. In specialty stores you can find EVOOs made from single varieties of olives, but the most widely available, and equally excellent—as well as less expensive—are blends. No two are alike; if you have the opportunity, try a few different brands to find the one you like best.

    Many cooks prefer a lighter-colored EVOO for cooking because it interacts more subtly with the flavors of other ingredients. (Contrary to what you may have heard, you *can* cook—even fry—with extra-virgin olive oil. Ignore all that nonsense about smoke points; at the temperatures your stove produces, the oil is unlikely to burn.) The bolder EVOOs, on the other hand, are great for drizzling on finished dishes for a dash of extra flavor.

- ***Virgin Olive Oil:*** Most, but not all, of the oil with this label also comes from the first pressing; some also comes from second or third pressings. Its flavor doesn't meet the same standards as EVOO, and it is a bit more acidic. Experts taste and test virgin oils to separate them into extra virgins and average virgins. You'd do perfectly well—though not quite as well—cooking with the less-expensive virgin as with extra virgin, but stick with EVOO for that ultimate finishing touch.

- ***Fino Olive Oil:*** This type of oil, a blend of extra virgin and virgin, is an option if you want to go a bit easier on your budget without compromising too much on flavor.

- **_Pure Olive Oil or Olive Oil:_** A blend of virgin and refined olive oil, this is the basic stuff used in mass-produced salad dressings and the like. It has only a little of the characteristic olive oil flavor and doesn't add much to a dish.

- **_Refined or Light Olive Oil:_** This oil is treated with chemicals and/or heat to remove its flavor. Some cooks like to use it for baking or deep-frying.

Spain produces more olive oil than any other country, but Italy exports more, so Italian olive oil is most prevalent on U.S. grocery shelves. Greece is the third of the big producers, while the presence of various other Mediterranean countries as well as California is growing. Which country makes the best oil? Only you can judge that for yourself. Spanish and Greek oil tends to be less expensive, and many of their olive oils are as good as Italian. The right choice is simply a matter of taste.

CHAPTER ONE

Tomato Sauces

Although tomatoes didn't exist in Italy until they arrived from the New World in 1548, they have become so central to Italian and especially Italian-American cooking that it's easy to think of them as the quintessential Italian ingredient. In the United States, old-school Italian-American restaurants are often called "red sauce joints," a testament to the iconic status to which the descendants of Italian immigrants have elevated the tomato. Tomato sauce appears in such ubiquitous dishes ranging from fried calamari to pizza, from eggplant parmigiana to spaghetti and meatballs.

From region to region, household to household, and season to season, Italians prepare a seemingly infinite variety of tomato sauces. But in truth you need know only two basic sauces, *pomodoro* and *marinara,* to be well equipped as you tackle Italian cooking. Debate rages among Italian food enthusiasts over the definitions of and distinctions—if any—between these two sauces. What is pomodoro sauce? What is marinara sauce? What is the difference? There are as many answers to these questions as there are Italians.

Here are two recipes that capture the general concept behind Italy's classic tomato sauces.

Marinara

MAKES 3½ CUPS

Marinara sauce is a simple preparation of chunky tomatoes and herbs. That's it. Since it contains so few ingredients, it's key to use the highest-quality canned tomatoes you can find after all, there's nothing in here to mask the mediocre flavor of substandard tomatoes. Look for the San Marzano variety (a number of Italian companies can and do export them), or if you can't find those, choose a good organic brand such as Muir Glen. Extra-virgin olive oil and fresh herbs are also essential. This really does make a difference! You will be rewarded with a light, fresh-tasting sauce that works wonderfully well on pasta, meat, and fish.

2 tablespoons extra-virgin olive oil
3 garlic cloves, minced
1 (28-ounce) can diced tomatoes
3 tablespoons fresh basil, minced
Salt and freshly ground black pepper

In a large saucepan over medium heat, heat oil and add garlic. Cook until garlic starts to sputter; do not brown it.

Add tomatoes, including the juice. Increase heat to medium-high and bring sauce to a boil. Reduce heat to simmer and cook, uncovered and stirring occasionally, until sauce thickens, about 15 minutes.

Add basil and season with salt and pepper. Cook for another 2 or 3 minutes.

Pomodoro Sauce

MAKES 3½ CUPS

Pomodoro *is the Italian word for* tomato. *Accordingly, sticklers say that the term* pomodoro sauce *describes any tomato sauce, in whatever form, but many cooks say that pomodoro sauce is a beast all its own, richer and more intense than marinara. This is a standard interpretation.*

....

¼ cup olive oil
2 garlic cloves, minced
1 small onion, chopped
2 small carrots, finely chopped
2 celery stalks, finely chopped
1 (28-ounce) can crushed tomatoes
1 (6-ounce) can tomato paste
1 dried bay leaf
1 teaspoon fresh oregano, chopped
1 teaspoon fresh basil, chopped
Salt and freshly ground black pepper

....

In a large saucepan over medium-high heat, heat oil and add garlic and onion. Sauté for about 10 minutes, until onion is translucent.

Add carrots and celery and sauté until soft, another 10 minutes. Pour in tomatoes, add tomato paste, and stir until paste dissolves into the sauce. Add herbs, season with salt and pepper, and stir well.

Bring sauce to a gentle boil; then reduce heat to low and cover. Simmer for 1 hour, stirring occasionally. If the sauce still seems too watery, uncover the pot and increase heat to medium. Cook, stirring, until sauce thickens to desired consistency.

Remove bay leaf and check seasoning. For a smoother texture, puree sauce in a blender or food processor.

CHAPTER TWO

Appetizers

Along with Spain, Italy is Europe's small-plates superstar. When served as appetizers, these meats, cheeses, vegetables, and olives make up a course called *antipasto*, a word that translates into English as "before the meal." An individual starter dish is also referred as an antipasto (plural, *antipasti*). Starters are generally served cold or at room temperature.

Antipasti usually appear only at big formal meals, when guests might nibble on small bites such as olives, nuts, and dips during cocktail hour and enjoy heartier offerings such as *salumi* (sliced cured meats, also called *affettati*); *formaggio* (cheese, plural *formaggi*); marinated, roasted, or grilled *verdure* (vegetables); and *bruschetta* or *crostini* (finger sandwiches), either buffet style or at the dinner table. Bread such as *ciabatta, focaccia,* or breadsticks often accompanies the antipasti.

Italian meals are as much social occasions as they are nutritional necessities. During the antipasto course everyone eats the same dishes, and the act of sharing food encourages people to connect with one another. Serving an appetizer slows down the meal, giving diners more time to chat and enjoy themselves. The slower pace, along with the lively colors and piquant flavors of the treats, wakes up the appetite and primes guests for the courses to come. A glass of wine or an *aperitivo* (aperitif) often accompanies the starting course, enhancing the effects of the food.

Many people eat Italian appetizers as an entire meal, and laying out an array of small, simple plates is an easy way to prepare a fun, delicious lunch or dinner. These dishes make an excellent accompaniment to wine; find a nice bottle of red, white, or rosé; light a candle; and get ready for a relaxing, no-fuss meal.

Salumi or Affettati (Cured Meat)

From bologna to salami, deli meat inspired by Italian cold cuts has long been a part of the American diet, especially in sandwiches. Today, imported Italian meats and faithful American renditions of them are readily available at deli counters. Ideally they are sliced as thinly as possible. The most familiar are:

- **Bresaola:** Lean beef that has been salted and air dried. It is deep red in color and somewhat sweet in flavor. Sliced paper thin, it is sometimes served on a bed of arugula and topped with some combination of olive oil, lemon juice, shaved Parmigiano-Reggiano, and black pepper.

- **Capicola:** Cooked cut pork shoulder or neck flavored with spices, herbs, and wine; stuffed into a casing; and hung up to dry. Often used in sandwiches.

- **Coppa:** Uncooked cut pork shoulder or neck flavored with spices, herbs, and wine; stuffed into a casing; and hung up to air dry. The sweet version is seasoned with black pepper; the hot version with red pepper. Often used in sandwiches.

- **Finocchiona:** A hard, dried salami made with coarsely ground pork and fennel seeds.

- **Genoa Salami**: Made with ground pork, a blend of pork and beef, or beef alone. Seasoned with salt, garlic, whole black peppercorns, and wine. Originated in America and was inspired by the sausage from the city of Genoa, Italy.

- **Mortadella**: A large, tender, cooked sausage made of very finely ground pork flecked with bits of pork fat and seasoned with black pepper. Sometimes studded with pistachios, it is mild in flavor and is the inspiration for American bologna. May be served sliced or cubed.

- **Pancetta:** Italian bacon made of pork belly, seasoned with salt and black pepper, rolled, and dry cured. More often used in cooking than as an antipasto.

- **Pepperoni:** An Italian-American salami made of highly seasoned ground beef and pork. Bright red and spicy, this is America's favorite pizza topping.

- **Prosciutto Crudo:** Uncooked, salted, air-dried pork or wild boar aged from nine months to two years. Varieties include prosciutto di Parma (Parma ham, produced only in the Parma region), sweeter and darker prosciutto di San Daniele (produced in the Friuli region), and American-made prosciutto. Sliced paper thin.

- **Prosciutto Cotto:** Cooked Italian ham, similar to American ham.

- **Salami:** The category of fermented, air-dried sausage that includes finocchiona, genoa, pepperoni, sopressata, and others. May be made of beef, pork, or game and spiced in a variety of ways. Generally has a coarse, dry texture. Distinct from salumi, the broader category of cured meats.

- **Sopressata:** Coarsely ground pork spiced, pressed, and air dried in a large casing. May be sweet (seasoned with black pepper) or hot (seasoned with red pepper). A type of salami.

- **Speck:** Smoked prosciutto from northernmost Italy, sometimes used like bacon. Not to be confused with German speck, which consists entirely of fat.

Formaggio (Cheese)

You may think of mozzarella, ricotta, Pecorino Romano, and Parmigiano-Reggiano as ingredients for baked pasta dishes or pizza, but they make excellent antipasti as well. Your antipasto platter can celebrate the vast world of Italian cheese, from the familiar provolone and gorgonzola to the hundreds of types you haven't heard of . . . yet. This list introduces you to some of the less-familiar antipasto-friendly varieties you'll find in your supermarket's gourmet cheese case or deli.

- **Asiago:** Hard cow's milk cheese from the Veneto region. Two varieties: The younger asiago pressato is mild, creamy, young, semi-firm, and good for melting; the aged asiago d'allevo is grainy, sharp, fruity, aged, and firm.

- **Bel Paese:** A mild, buttery, creamy cow's milk cheese. Pale yellow. Semi-soft, aged six to eight weeks. Sometimes substitutes for mozzarella.

- **Bocconcini:** Small egg- or ball-shaped forms of fresh mozzarella ranging in size from chicken eggs to marbles. Packaged in tubs with brine; sometimes marinated with olive oil and herbs.

- **Caciocavallo:** Like mozzarella and provolone, made by stretching the curd. Aged, salty, slightly sharp. Similar to provolone; melts well. Spherical in shape; may come waxed.

- **Fontina:** A pale yellow cheese made from raw cow's milk. Orange-brown rind, very aromatic, with a nutty/rich flavor. The aged version is hard, while the young version is semi-soft and excellent for melting. Good on pizza, in fondue, and for dessert.

- **Grana Padano:** A hard cheese with slightly sweet, robust flavor and grainy texture. Made from raw cow's milk, aged up to three years. Similar to Parmigiano-Reggiano.

- **Piave:** A hard yellow cow's milk cheese. Piave mezzano, aged three to six months, has a buttery, nutty flavor; piave vecchio, aged six to twelve months, is sharper and stronger, harder, and good for shaving and grating.

- **Taleggio:** A semi-soft, somewhat salty cow's milk cheese with a fruity tang and strong aroma. Good for melting.

Olives

Many Americans have discarded the belief that olives are just black, rubbery items that come in cans filled with salt water, or green, chewy, pimiento-stuffed things that come in jars (though martini-drinkers still love the green ones!). Those are made with mission olives from California and are eaten only in the United States, and they don't belong on your antipasto platter. Today most supermarkets have olive bars where you can find half a dozen or more varieties of this savory fruit. The assortment may include olives marinated with herbs or red pepper flakes, and some of the olives may be pitted. Depending on the variety, olives are picked at various stages of ripeness: less ripe olives are green, while riper olives are purple or black. They can't be eaten fresh off the tree (they're incredibly bitter), but must be cured in oil, water, brine, or salt. There are dozens of types of olives, many of them ideal for antipasto. Here are a few of the popular ones.

- **Cerignola**: A giant brine-cured olive, prepared in green, black, and red versions. Green is milder and firmer; black is more piquant and softer; red is similar to green, but dyed for the color. Green cerignolas are sometimes stuffed with garlic, blue or feta cheese, or pimientos.

- **Gaeta**: A small Italian olive that is either brine-cured (smooth-skinned, purple-brown) or oil-cured (wrinkled, black). Characterized by its mild, nutty flavor.

- **Kalamata or calamata**: Dark purple-black Greek olive that is meaty and almond-shaped. Cured in a vinegary brine; a rich and fruity flavor.

- **Liguria**: A zesty Italian black olive, brine-cured. Sometimes served with the stem on. Similar to Niçoise olives.

- **Manzanilla**: A green, brine-cured Spanish olive. Crisp and mild. Often stuffed with pimentos or garlic and used in martinis.

- **Moroccan**: A black olive from North Africa. Oil-cured or dry-cured, with wrinkled skin. Salty, with a somewhat bitter flavor and chewy texture.

- **Niçoise**: A petite, brownish-purple French olive with a big, mildly sour flavor. Brine-cured; large pits relative to the amount of meat. Famous as an ingredient in Salade Niçoise, the French classic.

- **Picholine**: A green, brine-cured French olive, often marinated with herbs de Provence. Understated, with a tart flavor and crisp texture.

- **Sicilian**: A fat, green Italian olive with solid, sour flesh. Brine cured and usually marinated with herbs.

Traditional Antipasto Platter

SERVES 6

If you've ever been to an Italian restaurant, you've encountered the antipasto platter. And if you've been to more than one Italian restaurant, you've encountered more than one version. As with every type of Italian food, the antipasto platter varies from region to region and from household to household. Typically it includes one or more meats, one or more cheeses, one or more marinated vegetables, some olives, and some bread. Sometimes there is also fruit or nuts. This version combines the best of the best. Of course, feel free to mix it up to suit your own tastes!

....

¼ pound prosciutto crudo, thinly sliced
¼ pound hot sopressata, thinly sliced
¼ pound chunk aged Asiago
¼ pound chunk Bel Paese
½ pound mixed cerignola, kalamata, and Moroccan olives
1 (6-ounce) jar marinated artichoke hearts, drained
6 ounces jarred, marinated whole mushrooms, drained
6 ounces jarred, pickled whole pepperoncini peppers, drained
1 (13-x-9-inch) loaf or 2 (12-inch-diameter) loaves plain, store-bought focaccia, cut
    into 1-x-4-inch pieces
Extra-virgin olive oil for dipping; buy the highest quality that you can afford

....

On a large serving platter, arrange the meats next to each other. Lay a serving fork on top.

Place the cheeses in center of the platter with a sharp knife for the asiago and a blunt knife for the bel paese.

Arrange the vegetables on the other side of the cheese with a serving fork.

Line a serving bowl or basket with a cloth napkin or tea towel, and put the focaccia in it.

Serve alongside 6 small, individual plates and a small bowl for the olive pits.

Alternatively, put meats and cheeses on a wooden or bamboo cutting board and the vegetables on a serving plate.

Vegetable Antipasto Platter

SERVES 6

Italians love the abundance of fresh, luscious produce that comes from their coun-tryside. Eggplant, zucchini, artichokes, peppers, asparagus, mushrooms, and a profusion of other vegetables not to mention tomatoes and olives (both fruit) take center stage at many a meal. Grilled and roasted, dressed with extra-virgin olive oil and marinated with herbs, drizzled with balsamic vinegar vegetables are celebrated in many forms. You can create a gorgeous antipasto platter with vegetables alone, either preparing them yourself or buying them premade at your supermarket.

....

Grilled or Roasted Vegetables

1 medium eggplant, ends cut off and globe sliced into ½-inch-thick rounds

1 medium zucchini, ends cut off and body sliced lengthwise into ½-inch-thick slabs

Kosher salt

1 large red bell pepper, seeded, de-ribbed, and cut into 1½-inch-wide strips

1 large orange bell pepper, seeded, de-ribbed, and cut into 1½-inch-wide strips

1 bunch asparagus (about 15 stalks), tough ends snapped off

½ cup extra-virgin olive oil

....

Preheat grill to medium or oven to 450°F.

Drizzle both sides of eggplant and zucchini slices with oil. Sprinkle one side with salt. In a large bowl, toss peppers and asparagus with olive oil and salt.

To Grill:

Brush or lightly coat grill rack with olive oil. Lay eggplant and peppers on the rack. Place peppers perpendicular to wires so they don't fall into the fire.

Cook eggplant until brown on one side and peppers until lightly charred on one side, about 5 minutes. Flip and cook on the other side until tender, about 5 min-utes. Remove vegetables to a plate and set aside.

Allow grill rack to reheat for about 3 minutes. Place zucchini and asparagus on the rack, perpendicular to wires. Cook zucchini until it has grill marks on one side, about 3 minutes. Flip and cook on the other side until tender, about 2 minutes.

Meanwhile, periodically roll asparagus on the rack to brown evenly on all sides. Cook until tender, about 5 minutes.

Remove vegetables to the plate with eggplant and peppers and allow to cool.

To Roast:

Line 2 baking sheets with foil. Pour about a tablespoon of oil onto each sheet and smear around to coat entire surface.

Lay vegetables in the pans, leaving space between pieces.

Place pans in the oven and roast for 10 minutes. Rotate the pans and continue roasting, checking every few minutes, until vegetables are tender. The eggplant and peppers will take about 20 minutes and the zucchini and asparagus about 15 minutes.

Remove pans from the oven and allow vegetables to cool.

Other Antipasto Items

½ pound mixed cerignola, kalamata, and Moroccan olives

1 (6-ounce) jar marinated artichoke hearts, drained

6 ounces jarred, marinated whole mushrooms, drained

6 ounces jarred, pickled cauliflower, drained

¼ cup jarred, sun-dried tomato pesto

⅓ cup crumbled feta

2 tablespoons balsamic vinegar

2 tablespoons fresh lemon juice

1 (13-x-9-inch) loaf or 2 (12-inch-diameter) loaves plain, store-bought focaccia, cut into 1-x-4-inch slices

Extra-virgin olive oil for dipping; buy the highest quality that you can afford

On a large serving platter, arrange all vegetables in a pleasing pattern, with contrasting colors next to each other.

Spread pesto on eggplant slices. Sprinkle feta over peppers. Drizzle zucchini with balsamic vinegar and asparagus with lemon juice.

Line a serving bowl or basket with a cloth napkin or tea towel and put focaccia in it.

Serve alongside 6 small, individual plates and a small bowl for olive pits.

Artichoke Caponata

SERVES 4

If you're familiar with caponata, the chunky Mediterranean bread topper made from a combination of vegetables and tomatoes, you probably think of eggplant, which is typically its main ingredient. This version replaces the eggplant with artichoke hearts and zips the antipasto up with Sicily's distinctive sweet-and-sour spicing.

....

¼ cup extra-virgin olive oil

1 small red onion, chopped

2 celery stalks, chopped

1 (9-ounce) package frozen artichoke hearts, thawed and chopped into
    ½-inch pieces

½ teaspoon salt, plus more for seasoning

½ teaspoon freshly ground black pepper

1 (14½-ounce) can diced tomatoes, drained

2 tablespoons tomato paste

10 large green olives (such as Sicilian), pitted and quartered

¼ cup golden raisins

2 tablespoons capers

¼ cup red wine vinegar

2 heaping tablespoons sugar

....

In a large skillet, heat oil over medium-high heat.

Add onion and celery, and sauté until onion is translucent, about 5 minutes.

Toss in artichoke hearts, ½ teaspoon salt, and pepper, and cook until artichoke hearts are tender and browned.

Add tomatoes, tomato paste, olives, raisins, and capers, and simmer for 5 minutes.

Stir in vinegar and sugar and cook to reduce the liquid so there's no runny juice left, about 1 minute. Add salt if desired and serve with sliced ciabatta bread.

Stuffed Mushrooms

SERVES 6

These savory bites taste a lot more difficult to make than they actually are. Your guests will be impressed when you bring out a tray full of them, and you'll be relaxed and ready to mingle. Stuffed mushrooms pair beautifully with light-bodied Italian red wine such as Bardolino, Valpolicella, and inexpensive Chianti.

....

24 medium (1½–2-inch-diameter) white or cremini mushrooms, soil brushed off
2 tablespoons olive oil
¼ cup pancetta or bacon, diced
2 garlic cloves, minced
¼ cup white onion, minced
¼ cup red bell pepper, finely chopped
1¼ cup bread crumbs
¾ cup fresh parmesan, grated, divided
¼ cup fresh Italian (flat leaf) parsley, chopped
Salt and freshly ground black pepper
2 tablespoons dry white wine (optional)
Extra-virgin olive oil for drizzling

....

Preheat the oven to 375°F.

Snap stems out of the mushroom caps. Set caps aside, and mince stems finely.

Heat oil in a large skillet and add minced stems, pancetta, garlic, onion, and pepper. Sauté until vegetables are tender and pancetta is slightly browned.

Transfer onion mixture to a large bowl. Add bread crumbs, ½ cup parmesan, and parsley, and season with salt and pepper. If mixture seems dry, add wine. All the bread crumbs should be moist to form a stuffing that holds together.

Line a baking sheet with foil, and spread on a light coating of oil.

Use your hands to fill caps with the stuffing and place on the pan. Drizzle mushrooms with extra-virgin olive oil and sprinkle with remaining 2 tablespoons of parmesan.

Bake until mushroom softens and topping turns a crispy golden brown, about 25 minutes. Serve warm.

Tomato and Basil Bruschetta

SERVES 6

Bruschetta *(pronounced* brusketta*), a Roman staple, is probably as old as the city itself. The traditional version is nothing more than bread toasted (preferably over a fire) and drenched in fresh green extra-virgin olive oil. Delectable on its own,* bruschetta *has evolved into many forms. This is the classic version, and so very simple to prepare.*

....

2 cups fresh, ripe tomatoes, coarsely chopped
3 tablespoons fresh basil, chopped
½ cup extra-virgin olive oil; buy the highest quality that you can afford
Coarse salt
1 (16–18-inch) loaf Italian bread, sliced about ¾ inch thick (20–24 slices)
2 cloves garlic

....

Preheat broiler or grill until very hot.

In a medium bowl, mix together tomatoes, basil, and 2 tablespoons oil. Set aside.

Place slices of bread under the broiler or on grill, and toast on both sides until pale brown. A little charring can add some flavor, but the bread should remain tender and moist inside.

Remove bread from heat and let cool until you can handle it. Rub one side of each slice with garlic, then brush with remaining oil.

Top the bread with the tomato mixture (leave the juice in the bowl) and serve immediately, before the bruschetta gets soggy.

Ricotta Crostini

SERVES 6

As simple as this recipe is, its delicate sweetness adds a layer of complexity to any Italian appetizer assortment. The honeyed tidbits provide a delightful contrast to the savory treats on your table and are a guaranteed hit with kids. Dress up the plate with quartered fresh figs, a stunning companion to ricotta. If you don't like nuts, you can replace them with diced peaches or thin slices of pear.

....

To make the toasts:

1 baguette, sliced ¼ inch thick

½ cup extra-virgin olive oil

Salt

....

Preheat the oven to 350°F.

Lightly brush or drizzle baguette slices with oil on both sides and place in a single layer on baking sheets. Sprinkle lightly with salt.

Toast bread in the oven until it turns light-golden brown, about 10 minutes. Turn slices over to toast other side, about 5 more minutes. The crostini should still be slightly tender inside, but not chewy.

Remove from oven and let cool in pan.

....

To make the crostini:

¾ cup walnut halves (about 2½ ounces)

1 (15-ounce) container fresh ricotta, room temperature

2 teaspoons fresh rosemary, finely chopped

⅓ cup clover honey

....

continued ▶

Arrange walnut halves on a baking sheet and toast in the oven 8–10 minutes, until aromatic and slightly darkened. Check frequently and shake the pan to keep nuts from burning. Remove from oven and let cool. Use your hands to break nuts into ¼-inch bits.

In a medium bowl, mix ricotta with the rosemary. With toast still on the baking sheets, drop about a tablespoon of ricotta onto each piece and spread to cover. Using a honey dripper or teaspoon, drizzle with honey, creating thin zigzags over the ricotta. Sprinkle evenly with walnuts. Arrange crostini on a serving platter.

Chicken Liver Crostini

SERVES 6

You may feel ambivalent about chicken liver or assume that you don't like it, but these little toasts spread with sweet, sumptuous pâté are a huge favorite in Tuscany. A few inexpensive ingredients combine into a creamy spread that seems downright luxurious.

....

2 tablespoons unsalted butter
½ cup extra-virgin olive oil, divided
1 garlic clove, minced
1 small white onion, finely chopped
2 teaspoons fresh sage, chopped
1 pound chicken livers, rinsed and patted dry
Salt and freshly ground pepper
⅓ cup dry Marsala, dry sherry, or cognac
Crostini, prepared as described in the Ricotta Crostini recipe

....

In a medium skillet over medium heat, melt butter with 2 tablespoons oil. Add garlic, onion, and sage and sauté until onion is tender and very lightly browned, about 6 minutes.

Increase heat to medium-high, add chicken livers, and season with salt and pepper. Cook until livers are brown one side, about 4 minutes, then flip over and brown the other side, 2 or 3 more minutes.

Reduce heat to medium and add wine or cognac. Break up livers with a fork or spoon while liquid reduces by half, about 5 minutes.

Remove from heat and transfer contents of skillet to a food processor or blender. Pulse until it reaches desired texture, chunky or smooth. Season with salt and pepper and cool to room temperature.

Spread pâté on the crostini and serve.

Prosciutto and Melon

SERVES 6

So refreshing, and refreshingly simple, this antipasto juxtaposes sweet and savory flavors, fatty and juicy textures. It makes a superb summer dish.

....

1 ripe cantaloupe, peeled, seeded, and cut into ½-inch-thick wedges
12 to 16 slices of prosciutto

....

Wrap one slice of prosciutto around each slice of melon. Place 2 or 3 pieces on each plate and serve.

Panfried Calamari

SERVES 4

Calamari (aka squid) can be a tricky ingredient: To avoid ending up with rubbery rings, you must cook it either very quickly or for a long time. This recipe, a much easier version of the fried calamari you find in restaurants, takes the first route to tender tastiness. You can buy precleaned fresh squid at your supermarket's fish counter.

....

¼ cup all-purpose flour

½ teaspoon salt

¼ teaspoon freshly ground black pepper

½ cup milk

Olive or canola oil for panfrying, about 1 cup

2 pounds fresh squid, cleaned and cut into ¼-inch rings and whole tentacle clusters, rinsed in cold water and patted dry

3 tablespoons fresh parsley, chopped

1 lemon, cut into 8 wedges

1 cup marinara sauce (see Chapter 1), warm

....

In a medium bowl, combine flour, salt, and pepper. Pour milk into a separate medium bowl. Place the squid into bowl with milk and moisten thoroughly. Shake excess milk off squid and transfer to the bowl with the flour mixture. Toss to cover lightly.

In a large skillet, heat about ⅓ inch oil over medium-high heat until very hot but not smoking. Distribute squid evenly in the skillet and fry, turning occasionally, until golden brown, about 6 minutes. Sprinkle parsley over the squid and toss.

Using a slotted spoon, remove squid from pan and drain for about 1 minute on a plate covered with paper towels.

Serve in bowls with lemon wedges and marinara sauce on the side.

Beef Spiedini

SERVES 4

In one form or another, meat on a stick is a popular dish around the world, and Italy loves it just as much as anyone else. The Italian version, thinly sliced beef coated with a bread-crumb mixture called modiga *and rolled up on skewers (*spiedini*), is especially tender and appetizing in its appearance.*

....

To make the *modiga*:

1½ cups plain bread crumbs

½ cup freshly grated parmesan

¼ cup fresh Italian (flat leaf) parsley, chopped

1 tablespoon fresh oregano, chopped

4 cloves garlic, minced

½ teaspoon salt

½ teaspoon freshly ground black pepper

....

In a medium bowl, combine all of the ingredients. Transfer to a plate and set aside.

....

To prepare the *spiedini*:

1½ pounds sirloin or top round, in a thick steak

½ cup olive oil

16–20 bay leaves

Toothpicks

....

Preheat broiler.

Slice steak crosswise into thin, 4-inch strips. Because you're going to roll them, the slices must be very thin, no more than ¼ inch thick and about half as wide (2 inches) as they are long. You may need to pound them to achieve this. To pound the meat, place each piece between plastic wrap and pound with a mallet or rolling pin until it reaches desired dimensions.

Rub each piece of meat on both sides with oil and press into the *modiga*. Roll up two pieces and skewer on a toothpick with a bay leaf sandwiched between them.

Place on a broiler pan. Broil the *spiedini* until lightly browned, 3–5 minutes per side.

CHAPTER THREE

Soups, Salads, and Egg Dishes

What cozier image could there be than that of an Italian grandmother putting a big bowl of steaming soup on the table? Italy's soups (*zuppe,* singular *zuppa*) are hearty, healing comfort food packed with seasonal vegetables and herbs, creamy beans, toothsome pasta, and tender meats. Because of the seasonality of their vegetables—the central ingredient in almost all of them—you can find a soup to suit every day of the year, whether it's a freezing winter night, a balmy Sunday in spring, a mellow summer evening, or a blustery autumn Tuesday. Like other Italian dishes, soup recipes vary from region to region: redolent of tomato and garlic in the south, bean-centric in the midsection, and rice-based and herbal in the north. Serve them with thick slices of crusty bread and they become satisfying meals unto themselves.

Italian salads (*insalata*) are equally seasonal and regional. Built from raw or cooked vegetables, sometimes layered with local cheese or herbs, occasionally integrating cured or raw meats, and delicately dressed with extra-virgin olive oil and a variety of excellent vinegars, they are packed with flavor. Even the most anti-salad diner will find something to love in these salads. Pair one of these plates with a bowl of soup to create a meal of exciting contrasts in flavor, texture, and temperature.

In Italy, egg dishes most often appear as antipasti rather than as breakfast food. Most often, breakfast (*colazione*) consists of a cup or two of piping hot espresso, cappuccino, or *caffè latte* (coffee with milk), sometimes paired with a pastry or a small prosciutto-and-cheese sandwich, and eaten while standing in a bar or *pasticceria* or bakery. At home, Italians might breakfast on simple cookies dipped in their coffee. The less typical, more elaborate breakfast might include some *salumi*, cheese, or fruit. For the most part, though, Italian breakfast is a sweet rather than savory meal; tourists are the only people who eat steak and eggs for breakfast (or drink cappuccino after 11 a.m.). But you're in America! Italian egg dishes are perfect for brunch, lunch, or a light dinner. Go for it!

Fresh Mozzarella

There are huge differences between fresh mozzarella and the bricks of off-white, shrink-wrapped stuff you're probably used to buying. That name-brand cheese is partially dried; hence the term "low-moisture" on the label. It's good for melting on pizza and in baked dishes such as *lasagne*, and kids like it in the form of string cheese. But for more delicate applications such as salad, you should use only fresh mozzarella. Fresh mozzarella comes in brilliant white balls of various sizes, most often as a large piece weighing about a pound. It may be sealed in plastic wrap or in a container of brine.

In Italy, mozzarella is sometimes made with buffalo milk, but *mozzarella di bufala* is expensive and a little difficult to find in the United States. But most American supermarkets now carry fresh *mozzarella fior di latte*, the more common variety, which is made from cow's milk. In contrast to its somewhat salty, firm, and grate-able low-moisture cousin (also made from cow's milk), fresh mozzarella is tender, a bit springy, and tastes like fresh, whole milk. It will keep only a week in the fridge, compared with up to a month for low-moisture mozzarella. It's perfect for salads, on its own, or on fancy pizza. Super-fresh mozzarella is so yummy that it'll disappear from your kitchen long before its expiration date!

Vinegar

Italy produces three types of vinegar that can really pump up the flavors of a salad. The two wine-based vinegars—red and white—are, at their best, aromatic and refined, tasting more of wine than of acetic acid (the main component of vinegar). They are sometimes infused with herbs such as tarragon and basil, aromatics such as garlic and fennel, spices such as chili, or fruit such as citrus and berries.

The king of Italian vinegar is neither white nor red, but brown. *Aceto balsamico,* or balsamic vinegar, is an elixir of balanced sweet and sour flavors. The real thing is made in the city of Modena from the juice of white wine grapes, which is boiled way down into *mosto cotto* ("cooked must") that is then fermented and aged in wooden casks to intensify the flavor. You won't see the authentic, officially certified version on your supermarket's shelves—it's aged at least twelve years and can cost $100 to $400 or more for a bottle—but you will have several brands and varieties from which to choose.

The cheapest of these, the mass-produced product labeled "Balsamic Vinegar of Modena," isn't true balsamic; it's made from wine vinegar that's artificially colored and thickened. If you can afford it, step up to the next level, *condimento balsamico*. At their most basic, these are made of wine vinegar with balsamic wine must added, and they aren't aged. As you go up the ladder in cost, the production method becomes more or less traditional, with the vinegars aged less than twelve years or not approved by Modena's balsamic guardians. The more age on the vinegar, the thicker, sweeter, and more potent it becomes. The *condimentos* are perfectly good for use on salads, although you won't want to use the best of them in salad dressing: They're meant for drizzling over antipasti, meat or fish dishes, or desserts. If you can, stock your pantry with a less-expensive *condimento balsamico* for salad dressing and a higher-quality one for adding flavor accents.

Minestrone

SERVES 6-8

Minestrone *falls into the category of* minestra, *or soups, which in centuries past were the food of the poor. Frequently,* minestra *served as their meal's only course, and in fact, minestrone can easily be a meal in itself. There is no set recipe for minestrone, but this one is a good example.*

....

3 tablespoons olive oil

1 medium onion, diced

4 garlic cloves, chopped

2 medium carrots, cut into ½-inch cubes

½ pound string beans, cut into 2-inch segments

3 stalks celery, cut crosswise into ¼-inch slices

1 large potato, peeled and cut into ½-inch cubes

½ small head of cabbage, chopped

2 small zucchini, cut into ½-inch cubes

½ pound fresh spinach, de-stemmed and coarsely chopped

2 (14½-ounce) cans diced tomatoes

1 (15-ounce) can cannellini beans

2 tablespoons fresh basil, chopped

2 tablespoons fresh Italian (flat leaf) parsley, chopped

6 cups beef broth

Salt and freshly ground black pepper

1 pound ditalini pasta, cooked per package directions and drained well

Freshly grated parmesan, for sprinkling

....

In a large pot over medium heat, heat oil and add onion, garlic, carrots, string beans, celery, and potato. Sauté for 10 minutes.

Add cabbage and zucchini and sauté for 5 more minutes. Add spinach and sauté for 3 minutes. Pour in tomatoes and beans, and add basil and parsley. Stir to mix, then pour in broth and stir again. Increase heat to high and bring soup to a boil.

continued ▶

Reduce heat to medium-low and simmer until vegetables are soft but still hold their shape, about 30 minutes. Season with salt and pepper.

Add ditalini and stir well, simmering soup for another 5 minutes. Ladle into bowls and serve with parmesan on the side.

Risi e Bisi

SERVES 4

A favorite spring soup in Venice, risi e bisi *(rice and peas) celebrates the season's fresh peas. You can prepare this recipe any time of year with frozen—not canned—peas, but it really is tastiest when made with fresh ones. Because it is made with arborio rice, the plump Italian rice used in risotto (see Chapter 6), many people confuse this dish with that, but authentic* risi e bisi *is a soup.*

....

4 tablespoons butter

4 shallots, finely chopped

2 ounces pancetta, diced

2 pounds fresh peas, shelled (can substitute one 16-ounce bag frozen peas, thawed)

5 cups chicken broth

2 cups arborio rice

½ cup freshly grated parmesan

2 tablespoons fresh Italian (flat leaf) parsley, chopped

Salt

....

In a medium pot over medium heat, melt butter, add shallots, and sauté until soft but not brown, about 5 minutes.

Add pancetta and cook until light brown. Stir in peas until coated with butter.

Add broth and rice, increase heat to medium-high, and bring soup to a gentle boil.

Reduce heat to medium so soup maintains a gentle boil, and cover pot. Cook, stirring occasionally, until rice is al dente, about 20 minutes.

Remove from heat, stir in parmesan and parsley, and adjust seasoning.

Wedding Soup

SERVES 6–8

When eating this soup, it's fun to envision a big Italian wedding, but the "wedding" in the name actually refers to the superb marriage of vegetable and meat flavors. Wedding soup is an Italian-American invention chock-full of little meatballs.

To make the meatballs:

½ pound ground beef

½ pound ground pork

1 large egg

2 tablespoons olive oil

⅓ cup fresh Italian (flat leaf) parsley, chopped

2 garlic cloves, grated

⅔ cup bread crumbs, more if needed

½ cup freshly grated parmesan,

¼ cup ricotta cheese

¾ teaspoon salt

¼ teaspoon freshly ground black pepper

Put all ingredients into a large bowl and combine thoroughly with your hands. If the mixture seems wet, add a little more bread crumbs. Scoop mixture a tablespoon at a time and roll between your hands to form balls about 1 inch in diameter. Place meatballs in a single layer on a baking sheet.

To prepare the soup:

3 tablespoons olive oil

1 medium onion, minced

4 garlic cloves, minced

2 stalks celery, minced

1 medium carrot, minced

2 tablespoons fresh basil, minced

3 quarts chicken broth

1 large head escarole, coarsely chopped

Salt and freshly ground black pepper

Freshly grated parmesan for sprinkling

In a large pot over medium-high heat, heat oil and add onion, garlic, celery, carrot, and basil. Sauté for about 10 minutes, until vegetables soften but do not brown.

Pour in broth and heat until it simmers rapidly. Cover and cook for 20 minutes.

Add escarole and continue to cook, uncovered, until greens are wilted and tender and soup reduces by about a third, about 30 minutes.

Carefully add meatballs and keep soup at a fast simmer until the meatballs cook through, about 20 minutes. Season with salt and pepper and serve with parmesan on the side.

Insalata Caprese

SERVES 4

Nothing says "summer" like fresh, vine-ripened tomatoes, especially if they come from your own garden. Here's a great, light way to use all that sweet and tangy plenty alongside subtle, creamy, fresh mozzarella.

....

4 medium, fresh slicing tomatoes, sliced ¼ inch thick

1 pound fresh mozzarella, sliced ¼ inch thick

1 bunch fresh basil

4 tablespoons extra-virgin olive oil

Coarse sea salt

....

On 4 individual salad plates, compose the salad by layering alternating slices of tomatoes and mozzarella in a circle that follows the shape of the plate.

Pluck basil leaves from the stems, and in bunches of about 10 leaves each, roll leaves together into a kind of herb cigar.

Chiffonade the basil by slicing cigar crosswise into very thin ribbons. Scatter the chiffonade over tomatoes and mozzarella.

Drizzle up to a tablespoon of oil onto each plate and finish with salt.

Insalata Mista

SERVES 6

*You could say that just about any salad (*insalata*) is mixed (*mista*). But a real Italian-style* insalata mista *combines as many colors, shapes, and flavors as you can find among the freshest vegetables in the produce aisle. The brilliance of the vegetables shines best when the salad is dressed simply with just a little extra-virgin olive oil and vinegar, but if you prefer you can also branch out with an herbed Italian dressing or a balsamic vinaigrette.*

....

6 stalks asparagus, woody ends snapped off
1 medium fennel bulb, tops and base cut off
2 small carrots, coarsely shredded or sliced into very thin rounds
1 large yellow bell pepper, seeded, de-ribbed, and cut lengthwise into thin strips
½ (14-ounce) can of artichoke hearts, rinsed, patted dry, and thinly sliced top
    to bottom
2 medium, ripe Roma tomatoes, cored and cut into thin wedges
⅓ cup extra-virgin olive oil, more if needed
¼ cup red wine vinegar, more if needed
Coarse sea salt and freshly ground black pepper
1 small head radicchio, sliced crosswise into very thin ribbons
1 small head Boston or Bibb lettuce, torn into bite-size pieces
1 small bunch or 1 (5-ounce) bag arugula, de-stemmed and torn into
    bite-size pieces

....

Cut tips off asparagus and place in a large mixing bowl. Using a vegetable peeler, shave stalks into the bowl as well.

Slice fennel crosswise into very thin discs. Use your hands to separate discs into rings, and put them in the bowl.

Add carrots, bell pepper, artichoke hearts, and tomatoes.

Pour in oil and vinegar and toss to coat. Season with salt and black pepper.

Add radicchio, lettuce, and arugula and toss thoroughly. Drizzle in a bit more oil, vinegar, or both if salad needs more dressing. Adjust seasoning as desired.

Insalata Tricolore

SERVES 4

Just like the Italian flag, this tricolor salad unfurls in green, white, and red splendor. But instead of the nation's plains (green), Alps (white), and heroes' blood (red), the hues of this vibrant dish bring to mind those of the nation's grand cuisine. In this version, a Dijon vinaigrette dresses up the vegetables.

....

To make the dressing:

⅓ cup extra-virgin olive oil

3 tablespoons fresh lemon juice

2 teaspoons Dijon mustard

1 garlic clove, cut lengthwise into thin slices

¼ teaspoon salt

⅛ teaspoon freshly ground pepper

....

In a small bowl, whisk together all ingredients. Set aside.

....

To prepare the salad:

1 large bunch or 2 (5-ounce) bags arugula, torn into bite-size pieces

2 large heads Belgian endive, ½ inch cut from base and remainder cut crosswise into ½-inch slices

1 medium head radicchio, torn into bite-size pieces

Salt and freshly ground black pepper (optional)

....

Put all ingredients into a large salad bowl.

Whisk vinaigrette again, remove garlic slices, pour half of the vinaigrette over salad and toss. If the salad needs more dressing, drizzle some into the bowl and toss until the salad is dressed to your liking.

Season with salt and pepper if desired.

Orzo Salad

SERVES 4

Orzo, a pasta shaped like large grains of rice, has just the right texture for a light, summery pasta salad.

....

To make the dressing:

3 tablespoons extra-virgin olive oil

Juice and zest of 1 large lemon

1 tablespoon fresh mint, minced

1 tablespoon fresh Italian (flat leaf) parsley, minced

Salt and freshly ground black pepper

....

In a small mixing bowl, whisk together oil, lemon juice and zest, mint, and parsley. Season with salt and pepper and set aside.

....

To prepare the salad:

1½ cups dry orzo, cooked al dente according to the package directions, to yield about 4 cups

1 large English cucumber (the kind wrapped in plastic), seeded and chopped into ½-inch pieces

⅔ cup feta cheese, crumbled

8 kalamata olives, pitted and quartered (optional)

Salt and freshly ground black pepper

....

In a large mixing bowl, combine orzo, cucumber, feta, and olives (if using).

Whisk the dressing again and add to the bowl. Toss all ingredients thoroughly and season as needed.

Panzanella

SERVES 4

This dish, a bread salad, might strike you as peculiar, but try it once and you'll be hooked. The poor of Tuscany invented it centuries ago to make use of every last stale crumb of bread, the cheapest of ingredients. Now, Italians of every class appreciate this economical creation. It's best by far when made with a sturdy, dense, rustic bread. If you can't find bakery-style country bread, use a crusty loaf of Italian or French bread (no sesame seeds) dried out (not toasted) in a 300°F oven for 5 to 10 minutes.

5 large, ripe tomatoes

1 medium loaf day-old or stale bread, cut into 1-inch cubes with the crust removed

Salt

1 garlic clove, minced

2 anchovy fillets, minced

1 tablespoon capers, minced

6 tablespoons extra-virgin olive oil

3 tablespoons red wine vinegar

½ medium red onion, chopped

1 medium yellow bell pepper, seeded, de-ribbed, and chopped into ¼-inch pieces

1 cup English cucumber (the kind in the plastic wrap), chopped

1 small bunch fresh basil, de-stemmed and torn into ¼-inch pieces

Core tomatoes and chop coarsely. Remove most of the seeds and put chunks of flesh into a sieve over a medium bowl to drain; reserve juice.

In a large mixing bowl, toss bread (including crumbs) with the tomato juice and ¼ teaspoon salt. Allow to steep for about 15 minutes, tossing occasionally, until bread is moist but not wet.

In a small mixing bowl, combine garlic, anchovies, capers, oil, and vinegar. Mash into a smooth consistency. Add onion, pepper, cucumber, and basil to the bread mixture and toss. Pour in the dressing, toss, and season with salt. The bread should be saturated and partially dissolved to a grainy paste consistency.

Tortino di Spinaci

SERVES 6

The Italian version of a quiche, this dish is an easier take on the classic sformato, *or* flan. *Firm, warm, and custardy, it's an excellent brunch dish, though Italians tend to serve it as an antipasto.*

....

2 teaspoons salt, divided

3 pounds fresh spinach, or 2 (10-ounce) boxes frozen spinach, thawed and liquid squeezed out

6 large eggs

1¼ cup whole milk

4 tablespoons freshly grated Pecorino Romano cheese

1 pinch nutmeg, ground

3 tablespoons butter

1 cup bread crumbs

....

Preheat the oven to 375°F.

To cook the spinach:

If using fresh spinach: In a large pot over high heat, mix 1 teaspoon salt with about a gallon of water. Bring to a boil.

Fill a large mixing bowl about two-thirds full with cold water and two trays of ice cubes.

Blanch about 1 pound spinach by boiling it for 30 seconds to 1 minute, until it turns bright green.

Immediately remove from the water with a slotted spoon, allowing the hot water to drip back into the pot, and plunge into the ice water to stop cooking. When cool, remove from the water and squeeze out excess.

Repeat for the remaining 2 pounds of spinach using the same water, replenishing as necessary with additional water and ice.

To prepare the *tortino*:

Coarsely chop blanched or thawed spinach.

In a large mixing bowl, beat eggs and beat in milk, cheese, nutmeg, and ½ teaspoon salt. Add spinach and mix thoroughly.

Butter a 9-inch pie pan with 1 tablespoon butter. Melt the other 2 tablespoons butter and, in a small mixing bowl, toss with the bread crumbs and the remaining ½ teaspoon of salt.

Press bread crumbs onto sides and bottom of the pan to form a crust. Place pan on a baking sheet.

Pour spinach-and-egg mixture into the pan. Slide baking sheet with the pan into the oven and bake for about 30 minutes or until a knife inserted in the center comes out clean.

Remove from oven and let cool 5 minutes before cutting into 6 wedges.

Fritatta with Herbs

MAKES 1 FRITTATA (1 MAIN-COURSE SERVING)

This extremely versatile dish is essentially a thin, circular, open-faced omelet. Instead of adding the fillings after the eggs have partially cooked, mix all of the ingredients together before pouring them into the pan. Improvise with ingredients: Just about any meat, vegetable, or cheese will work in a frittata. You can serve it at any temperature (except right out of the fridge); cut it into pieces for an antipasto; or eat it whole as a main course at breakfast, brunch, lunch, or a light dinner. Green salad is an ideal accompaniment.

....

2 large eggs
2 tablespoons milk
¼ teaspoon salt
Pinch of freshly ground black pepper
1½ teaspoons fresh basil, chopped
1½ teaspoons fresh parsley, chopped
1 teaspoon fresh chives, chopped
1 teaspoon fresh thyme, chopped
1 teaspoon fresh sage, chopped
1 teaspoon olive oil
1 teaspoon unsalted butter

....

Preheat broiler.

In a small mixing bowl, whisk together eggs, milk, salt, and pepper. Stir in fresh herbs until blended. In a small ovenproof skillet, heat oil and butter over medium-high heat until butter melts and fat starts to foam.

Stir eggs again and pour into the skillet. Reduce heat to very low and cook until eggs are set but top is still runny, 3 to 4 minutes.

Slide skillet under the broiler and cook until top of frittata sets and browns very slightly, about 1½ minutes.

continued ▶

VARIATION: PROSCIUTTO AND ASPARAGUS

....

2 slices prosciutto, cut crosswise into ¼-inch strips
2 stalks asparagus, woody end chopped off and tender part cut into 1-inch pieces

....

Steam the asparagus for 2–3 minutes, until bright green and tender, but still crisp. Prepare frittata as earlier, omitting the basil, parsley, and chives.

VARIATION: TOMATO AND FETA

....

1 medium tomato, coarsely chopped, seeds removed and juice drained
¼ cup crumbled feta cheese

....

Prepare the frittata as earlier, omitting parsley, chives, thyme, and sage.

VARIATION: ZUCCHINI AND PARMIGIANO-REGGIANO

....

½ small zucchini, thinly sliced
¼ cup freshly grated Parmigiano-Reggiano

....

In a small skillet over medium heat, heat a teaspoon of oil.

Sauté zucchini until it starts to soften. Remove to a paper towel to cool, leaving olive oil behind.

Prepare frittata as earlier, omitting basil, parsley, and chives; do not add more oil to skillet.

CHAPTER FOUR

Sandwiches, Panini, and Pizza

Bread has always had a prominent place on the Italian table, and it appears in one form or another at every meal. So it's no surprise that Italians often combine it with other parts of the meal—meat, vegetables, cheese, sauce, olive oil—to create sandwiches and pizza. Modern realities have made the sandwich more popular than ever in Italy, as the always growing demands of the workplace have required people to eat more of their meals away from home. Sandwiches and pizza are easy to eat standing up in a bar or bakery, on short meal breaks, or whenever people can't sit down for a meal. But quick, handheld meals in Italy are for the most part as fresh and tasty as a three-course meal.

Italian sandwiches are different from American sandwiches. Instead of sliced bread or hero rolls overstuffed with everything from pulled pork to roasted turkey breast, pickles to shredded lettuce, and slathered with mayonnaise, mustard, and just about any other condiment you can think of, sandwiches in Italy highlight hearty, crusty bread. Sandwiches are small and lightly filled with just a slice or two of prosciutto, salami, provolone, or tomato. Rarely are there more than two ingredients, plus a delicate smear of mayo, butter or garlic, and maybe some herbs, between the bread.

In the United States, immigrants transformed the notion of the Italian sandwich into the fat hero crammed with multiple deli meats, cheeses, hot peppers, and dressings. The Italian-American hero—aka sub, grinder, hoagie, po' boy, etc.—is a noble thing that literally bursts with bold flavors. It's as truly American as apple pie.

So is the American-style *panini,* the flat, pressed sandwich, served hot or cold, that suddenly appeared across the country in the 1980s and 1990s. They take their inspiration from Italian panini (singular *panino*), although in Italy panini (translation, "rolls") are sandwiches made on rolls such as ciabatta or baguette instead of sliced bread. Like their American cousins they are pressed and sometimes served warm. In the United States, panini may be piled high with fillings or even constructed as double or triple-deckers, and they are as often made on sliced bread as on rolls. Sandwiches on sliced bread are called *tramezzini* (sandwiches) in Italy, or, if toasted, simply called "toasts."

There are just as many differences between another bread-based Italian staple—pizza—and its American offshoots. The dish originated in the southern Italian city of Naples, as inexpensive food for the poor. As far back as ancient Roman times, people had been making flatbreads topped with olive oil, cheese, and other locally available ingredients. When the tomato arrived from the Americas in the sixteenth century, it became a common topping in Southern Italy, and from there, the classic Neapolitan pizza evolved.

Italian immigrants introduced America to pizza in the nineteenth century. It developed into a uniquely American dish in the northeastern states, where many Italian immigrants settled. Workers ate the easily portable food in the morning as well as on their breaks later in the day, and pizzerias started selling slices to those who couldn't afford, or didn't want, whole pies. Pizzerias soon popped up in cities across the country and, in the decades following World War II, pizza skyrocketed in popularity to become one of America's favorite foods.

Like sandwiches, Italian pizza tends to highlight the crust, sparingly topped with only a few ingredients. Mainstream American pizza is more topping-centric, with a far greater variety and quantity of ingredients piled on top of the crust. Chicago took the approach even farther, with the invention of the deep-dish pizza that more closely resembles the filled American dessert pie than thin flatbread. But in the twenty-first century, Americans have started to rediscover more traditional Italian pizza. *Pizzaioli* (pizza chefs) have been using traditional Italian techniques and ingredients to make more authentic crusts, and topping them with fewer, more authentic ingredients and more sophisticated innovations. It's an exciting trend that opens a world of possibility to pizza lovers. Nevertheless, the mouthwateringly greasy slice, whether topped with pepperoni or Buffalo-style chicken, is alive and well and, true to its origins, American pizza remains a relatively inexpensive convenience food.

Tuna and Egg Tramezzini

SERVES 4

The dainty Venetian tea sandwiches known as tramezzini *(singular* tramezzino*)
are usually eaten as an afternoon snack or early evening nibble. Assembled on
slender, triangular slices of white bread, crusts removed, they may be filled with a
little prosciutto with arugula, smoked salmon with cucumber, cheese with tomato, or
other simple fillings. This recipe is for the most classic of all tramezzini. For the most
authentic results, find a good firm, white sandwich bread that's sliced thin and a jar
of Italian tuna in oil. If you can't find the Italian tuna, American tuna in oil will do.*

1 (7-ounce) jar Italian tuna in oil, drained

2 tablespoons capers, roughly chopped

2 tablespoons kalamata olives, roughly chopped

2–3 tablespoons mayonnaise, depending on your taste, plus more for spreading

Salt and freshly ground black pepper

8 thin slices white bread, crusts removed

3 large eggs, boiled for 6–8 minutes, peeled, and sliced crosswise into
6 slices each

In a medium mixing bowl, break tuna into small flakes. Add capers, olives, and
mayonnaise and mix well, until tuna has a smooth consistency. Season with salt
and pepper, and refrigerate.

Cut each slice of bread into 4 triangles of equal size. Spread 8 of the triangles with
thin layer of mayonnaise.

Place one slice of egg on each of the dressed triangles. Drop about a tablespoon
of the tuna mixture onto each egg slice, and spread thinly to cover entire triangle.
Place an undressed triangle of bread on top of the tuna, and press down lightly
to seal.

Put the sandwiches on a serving dish and refrigerate, covered with a slightly damp
cloth, for 30 minutes before serving.

Muffaletta

SERVES 2–4

Invented by Italian immigrants in New Orleans, the muffaletta sandwich has become a symbol of that city. It is named for the bread with which it's made: a round, flat, fairly soft Sicilian loaf about 10 inches in diameter and topped with sesame seeds. It's a big sandwich, so it's cut into quarters to feed two big appetites or four smaller ones. If you can't find muffaletta bread, you can substitute regular seeded Italian bread. Another main ingredient is a kind of chopped olive salad that you should be able to find in jars in the condiment section of your supermarket. If there's none available, you can make it using the recipe below.

To make the olive salad:

1 cup pimento-stuffed olives, sliced, plus 2 tablespoons liquid from the jar

1 cup giardiniera (pickled celery, cauliflower, and carrot), chopped, plus 1 tablespoon liquid from the jar

½ cup kalamata olives, pitted and sliced

2 tablespoons capers, plus 1 tablespoon liquid from the jar

1 tablespoon jarred pepperoncini peppers (without seeds), chopped

1 tablespoon garlic, minced

2 teaspoons dried oregano

1 teaspoon dried parsley

¼ cup extra-virgin olive oil

In a medium mixing bowl, combine all ingredients and mix well. Refrigerate for at least an hour before using; the salad is even better if you let it marinate overnight.

To assemble the muffaletta:

1 loaf muffaletta bread, or 1 large loaf seeded Italian bread

¼ pound low-moisture mozzarella, sliced

¼ pound mortadella, sliced

¼ ounces capicola, sliced

¼ pound Genoa salami, sliced

¼ pound mild provolone cheese, sliced

Slice bread horizontally and open the loaf. Spread each half generously (about ¼ inch deep) with the olive salad. (You will probably have leftover salad; it will keep in the fridge, tightly sealed, for up to two weeks.)

Lay the mozzarella on the bottom piece of bread, covering entire surface; then layer the meats. Lay the provolone on the top piece of bread, covering entire surface.

Quickly turn top over onto the bottom, being careful not to lose any of the cheese or olives.

Seal sandwich in plastic wrap and let rest for 30 minutes to allow bread to soak up some of the salad juices.

Cut sandwich into quarters and serve.

Sausage and Peppers on Italian Bread

SERVES 4

This heavy sandwich staple of American pizzerias, street fairs, and Italian neigh-borhoods actually has deep roots in Italy. There, its filling appears in trattorias and home-cooked meals as a main course, with bread on the side. Fresh, high-quality ingredients elevate this sandwich to gourmet status.

¼ cup olive oil, divided
2 hot Italian sausages
2 sweet Italian sausages
1 large onion, halved then sliced crosswise into ¼-inch-wide crescents
1 green bell pepper, seeded, de-ribbed, and cut into ¼-inch-wide strips
1 red bell pepper, seeded, de-ribbed, and cut into ¼-inch-wide strips
1 yellow bell pepper, seeded, de-ribbed, and cut into ¼-inch-wide strips
4 garlic cloves, slivered
1 (15-ounce) can crushed tomatoes
Salt
1 (16–18-inch) loaf Italian bread

In a large skillet, heat 1 tablespoon oil over medium heat and add sausages. Brown them slowly, occasionally turning over so they brown on all sides.

Remove sausages from skillet and set aside for 10 minutes to absorb their juices. Pour any excess fat out of the skillet.

Place skillet over medium-high heat and add remaining oil, heating until it is just short of smoking. Scrape the brown bits off the bottom of the pan as you continue cooking. Add the onion and sauté until it is slightly browned, about 15 minutes.

Increase heat to high and add peppers. Sauté, stirring frequently, until they soften and sear, taking on a few blackened spots. Reduce heat to medium-high, add garlic, and cook for another 2 minutes. Stir in tomatoes and continue cooking.

Slice the sausages in half lengthwise, cut the halves in half, and return them to the skillet. Bring the contents to a simmer, turn the heat to medium, and simmer until the liquid reduces slightly and the sausages cook through, about 20 minutes.

Cut bread crosswise into 4 equal pieces. Halve each piece horizontally and open it. Transfer the sausage, peppers, and onions to the sandwiches, and spoon the sauce over the top.

Prosciutto and Fontina Panini

SERVES 4

With a bit more filling than the Italians use in their panini, this version is still stuffed lightly enough to cook through and won't make a mess when the cheese melts. A two-sided electric griddle or panini press will make your job easier and yield somewhat better results, but you can make equally fabulous panini without investing in one.

....

1 (12 to 14-inch) loaf ciabatta, sliced horizontally into a sandwich top and bottom
8 thin slices fontina (about ¼ pound)
4 very thin slices red or Vidalia onion (optional)
Freshly ground black pepper
8 thin slices prosciutto (about ¼ pound)
1 tablespoon extra-virgin olive oil

....

Preheat panini press (if using) to medium heat.

Open ciabatta, cut sides up. Lay 4 slices of fontina on bottom piece of ciabatta, covering the bread end-to-end but not allowing the cheese to extend past its edges. Putting the cheese on the bread before the prosciutto helps bind the panino together. Place the onion slices on top of the cheese, spacing them evenly. Sprinkle with pepper. Lay the prosciutto over the onions to cover the cheese—don't let it hang over the edge of the bread. Place the remaining 4 slices of fontina on top, follow with the top piece of bread, and press it down to secure.

If you are not using a panini press, heat a stove-top griddle or large skillet over medium-high heat. If your griddle has a ridged side, place that side up.

Lightly brush outsides of panino with olive oil.

Put the sandwich on the press, on a stove-top griddle, or in the skillet. (You may need to cut into two panini to make it fit.) Close the press, or lay foil over the panini in the skillet and put a heavy, flat-bottomed skillet or pot on top. To flatten the sandwiches, push down on the top of the press or on the top skillet.

Cook the panino or panini until the bottom side turns golden-brown, about 4 minutes, then turn over and cook the other side another 4 minutes, with the panini press closed or foil and skillet on top. Cook until the second side turns golden-brown and the cheese is melted.

Cut the whole panino into four even pieces, or the two panini in half.

Grilled Vegetable Panini

SERVES 4

Sweet and succulent, grilled veggie panini are not for vegetarians only. The juice of the vegetables and the oil in the pesto soak into the bread, heightening the lusciousness. If you like, add some provolone for variety.

....

To make the pesto:

¼ cup pine nuts (pignoli)

2 packed cups fresh basil leaves

2 garlic cloves, chopped

6 tablespoons freshly grated Parmigiano-Reggiano or Romano cheese

6 tablespoons extra-virgin olive oil, more or less if needed

Salt

....

Put pine nuts in a food processor or blender and pulse a few times to make crumbs. Add basil and garlic and pulse several times to chop finely into a dry paste. Add the cheese and pulse to blend. Drizzle in about a tablespoon of the olive oil and turn on the machine. While the machine runs, pour in the oil in a thin stream. Stop a few times to scrape down the sides of the bowl, so all of the ingredients blend evenly. Keep adding oil until the pesto is a smooth paste the density of deli mustard or mayonnaise. Season with salt and blend for 30 more seconds.

....

To prepare the panini:

1 large portobello mushroom

1 medium zucchini, sliced lengthwise into ¼-inch slabs

1 medium red bell pepper, seeded, de-ribbed, and cut into 1½-inch-wide slices

1 (12 to 14-inch) loaf ciabatta, sliced horizontally into a sandwich top and bottom

½ cup pesto, ready-made or prepared from the preceding recipe

Salt and freshly ground black pepper

....

Grill the vegetables according to the instructions in the Vegetable Antipasto Platter recipe in Chapter 2. Leave the portobello mushroom whole while grilling; then slice into ¼-inch slabs.

Open the ciabatta, cut sides up. Spread each side completely with ¼ cup of the pesto. Lay the portobello slices on the bottom piece of bread, covering the entire surface. Place the zucchini slabs on top of the portobello, spacing evenly. Season with salt and pepper. Layer on the peppers to cover all of the zucchini. Close the sandwich with the top piece of bread.

Toast the outsides of the panino according to the instructions in the preceding Prosciutto and Fontina Panini recipe, and cut into 4 panini of equal size.

Pizza Crust

Pizza fans know that a great pizza has as much to do with the crust as with the top-pings. Follow this recipe exactly to make the perfect crust. These instructions are for making the dough by hand; you can use a standing kitchen mixer or food processor instead, but be careful not to over-process the dough. Your crust will be best if you make the dough at least 24 hours in advance. If you don't have the time to make your own dough, you can also buy ready-made pizza dough in the refrigerator or freezer aisle of your supermarket (though it's not as good). Stay away from prebaked crusts, as they are too bready and chewy to make a good Italian- or New York style pizza.

....

1½ cups warm (100–110°F) water, plus more if needed

1 packet (2½ teaspoons) active dry yeast

2 tablespoons sugar

3 cups all-purpose flour, plus more for adjusting recipe and sprinkling work
    surfaces

2 tablespoons olive oil, plus more for greasing bowls, pans, and crust

1 teaspoon salt

....

Before you start mixing, make sure the water is the correct temperature: Too cool or too warm, and the yeast won't work.

In a large mixing bowl, thoroughly combine water, yeast, sugar, and ½ cup of the flour. Let sit in a warm place for 20 minutes. If it doesn't get bubbly, the yeast is not working and you must discard the mixture and start over again.

Add the oil and salt to the liquid, and slowly add 2 cups of the flour, mixing with a large wooden spoon just until the dough forms a soft, slightly sticky ball. If the dough is too dry, add a little more water; if it is too wet, add a bit more flour. Using your hands—not a surface—form the dough into a ball. Handle the dough as little as possible so it doesn't get tough (and make a tough crust).

Lightly grease another large mixing bowl with oil and put in the dough. Roll the ball around to cover it with oil. Cover the bowl loosely with plastic wrap or a clean kitchen towel, and place the bowl in a warm spot until the dough doubles in size, 1½–2 hours.

Lightly flour a work surface. Punch down the dough once or twice in the bowl and use your hands (not the surface) to gently shape it into a ball (if you are making one large pizza) or 2 equal-size balls (if you are making 2 small pizzas). Put the dough on the floured surface, sprinkle with flour, and cover it with plastic wrap or a towel. Let the dough rest until it puffs up a little, about 20 minutes.

If you plan to set the dough aside for a few hours or overnight, wrap it tightly in plastic wrap and put it in the refrigerator. Before using the dough, let it warm back up to room temperature.

For a large rectangular pizza: Use about 1 teaspoon oil to grease a 13-×-18-inch baking sheet. Put the dough on the pan and press and stretch it by hand—not with a rolling pin—almost to the full dimensions of the pan. The crust will be very thin; make sure it is an even thickness throughout.

For two round pizzas: Use about 1 teaspoon of oil to grease each of two 13-×-18-inch baking sheets. Put a ball of dough on each pan and press and stretch it by hand—not with a rolling pin—into a 12- to 14-inch round. It's okay if the crusts are irregularly shaped, as long as they are an even thickness throughout.

Lightly drizzle a little olive oil on the crust and spread it around with your fingers. Now, build your pizza!

Makes 1 (13-×-18-inch) rectangular crust or 2 (12- to 14-inch) round crusts.

Pizza Margherita

SERVES 4

Simply delicious, this pie relies on only a few ingredients to produce an Italian icon, so spring for the very best ingredients you can find: imported San Marzano or domestic organic tomatoes (they really do taste better!), super-fresh mozzarella, young (small) basil leaves, sea salt, and the finest extra-virgin olive oil you can afford.

....

Pizza crust, prepared according to the Pizza Crust recipe
2 cups canned, crushed San Marzano or organic tomatoes
12 ounces fresh mozzarella, cut into ¼-inch-thick slices
16 small basil leaves
2 tablespoons extra-virgin olive oil
Sea salt

....

Move one oven rack to the lowest rung and one to the highest. Preheat the oven to 500°F.

Spread tomatoes uniformly across the crust. Distribute mozzarella slices. Scatter basil evenly over the top. Drizzle oil over the basil. Salt lightly.

If cooking one pizza, slide pan onto the lowest oven rack. If cooking two pies on two pans, place one pan on each oven rack. Cook until the bottom of the crust is golden brown and the cheese is bubbling, 10 to 12 minutes. If using two pans, switch them between the shelves every 3 minutes, opening the oven door as briefly as possible.

Immediately slide the finished pizza onto a large cutting board. Cut a large rectangular pie into 8 even pieces and a 12-inch round pie into 4 pieces, and serve immediately.

Pizza Marinara

SERVES 4

The simplest of the Italian pizzas, pizza marinara is traditionally made only with tomatoes, garlic, oregano, and extra-virgin olive oil, without any mozzarella or other toppings. You can still find the cheese-free version at some old-school pizzerias in the northeastern United States, but most Americans prefer their pizza marinara with mozzarella and any number of toppings. In Rome, pizzaioli add a few anchovies and call it pizza alla napoletana, *while the people of Naples, (where any pizza is, by definition,* alla napoletana*) call it* alla romana. *You might call this recipe pizza alla americana.*

Pizza crust, prepared according to the Pizza Crust recipe
2 cups marinara sauce (see page 2)
2 small garlic cloves, slivered
1 tablespoon fresh oregano, chopped, or 1 teaspoon dried
2 tablespoons extra-virgin olive oil
12 ounces low-moisture mozzarella, shredded
Sea salt

Move one oven rack to lowest rung and one to highest. Preheat the oven to 500°F.

Spread marinara sauce uniformly across the crust. Scatter garlic and oregano evenly over the sauce. Drizzle oil over the herbs. Top with cheese.

Cook as directed in recipe for Pizza Margherita.

Toppings

Americans love their pizza toppings. Endlessly creative and individualistic, they have wandered far from the Italian nest of ingredients. Raisins, corned beef, tater tots, bean sprouts, ranch dressing, whatever—if it's edible, it shows up on American pizza. Overloaded pizzas: supreme, meat-lovers, veggie-lovers, extra cheese, extra sauce, etc. are big hits all over the United States. Purists cringe at the orgy and declare that these pies don't qualify as pizza, but America is a revolutionary place

continued ▶

where no one can tell pizza fans what they can and cannot do. Here are some traditional and not-so-traditional ingredients you might want to add to your Pizza Marinara. Note that pizzas with a lot of toppings may take longer to cook.

Anchovies
Artichoke hearts
Arugula
Asiago
Bacon
Barbecued chicken
Basil
Bell peppers (any color)
Black olives (any variety)
Broccoli
Broccoli rabe
Buffalo chicken
Calamari
Cheddar
Chives
Clams
Colby
Eggplant
Eggs (cracked on midway
    through cooking)
Fennel
Feta
Fresh mozzarella
Fresh tomatoes (any variety)
Freshly ground black pepper
Goat cheese
Green olives (any variety)
Ground beef
Ham (any variety)
Hot chili flakes
Hot peppers (any variety, fresh
    or pickled)

Hot sauce
Kale
Manchego
Meatballs (any variety)
Mexican cheese (any variety)
Monterey jack
Mushrooms (any variety)
Onions (raw or cooked)
Parmigiano-Reggiano
Pecorino Romano
Pepperoni
Pesto
Pineapple
Potato slices
Prosciutto
Provolone
Ricotta
Salami (any variety)
Salsa
Sausage (any variety)
Scallions
Shallots
Shredded beef
Shredded chicken
Smoked mozzarella
Spinach
Sun-dried tomatoes
Truffles
Zucchini

Pizza Quattro Stagioni

SERVES 4

The name of this traditional Italian pizza translates as "four seasons pizza." It's topped with ingredients that represent each of the four seasons, each ingredient covering a quarter of the pie. There are many interpretations of this dish; this one is fairly common.

....

Pizza crust, prepared according to the Pizza Crust recipe

3 tablespoons extra-virgin olive oil, divided

2 cloves garlic

¾ cup white, button, or cremini mushrooms (winter), sliced

2 cups marinara sauce (see page 2)

12 ounces fresh mozzarella, diced into ¼-inch pieces

¼ cup freshly grated Parmigiano-Reggiano or Pecorino Romano

½ cup artichoke hearts (spring), roughly chopped

½ cup kalamata olives, pitted and quartered (summer)

4 ounces prosciutto, sliced and cut crosswise into ¼-inch-wide ribbons (fall)

....

Preheat the oven to 500°F.

In a medium skillet over medium heat, heat 1 tablespoon olive oil. Add garlic and mushrooms and sauté until mushrooms soften, about 4 minutes. Set aside.

Spread marinara sauce evenly over the crust, leaving a ¼-inch border of uncovered dough. Scatter mozzarella across pizza, then grated cheese.

Use a knife to lightly mark surface of the pizza with boundaries between 4 equal quarters; do not cut. Put mushrooms, artichokes, olives, and prosciutto into separate quarters. Drizzle pizza with 2 tablespoons oil.

Cook as directed in recipe for Pizza Margherita.

Slice each "season" into 4 pieces; serve 1 piece of each season per person.

Pizza Bianca

SERVES 4

The best white pizza isn't just pizza without tomato sauce. Yes, you can make a white pie by using a few types of cheese and no tomato sauce, but you'll get a tastier pizza bianca if you replace the red sauce with white sauce, a thickened dairy-based sauce that lends a velvety richness to the pie. Here is a time-honored recipe for pizza bianca; if you want to add toppings, try basil, spinach, artichoke hearts, or prosciutto.

To make the white sauce:

1 cup whole milk

2 tablespoons unsalted butter

2 tablespoons all-purpose flour

¼ teaspoon salt

¼ teaspoon black pepper

4 cloves garlic, minced

1 teaspoon fresh thyme, minced

In microwave, heat milk on high until steaming, about 30 seconds (time will vary according to your microwave's power). Leave in microwave.

In a medium-small saucepan on low heat, melt butter until it foams and then stops foaming. Add flour a little at a time and stir constantly until the mixture is smooth. Add milk slowly and steadily, in a thin stream, and whisk to thoroughly combine ingredients. Keep whisking while adding salt and pepper; then increase heat to medium. Whisk steadily, until sauce comes to a boil and thickens.

Remove from heat and whisk in the garlic and thyme. Immediately pour sauce into a blender and blend until smooth, about 15 seconds. Pour sauce into a bowl and cover with plastic wrap. Set aside.

To make the pizza:

Pizza crust, prepared according to the Pizza Crust recipe

1 cup part-skim ricotta

1 teaspoon fresh oregano, chopped

¾ cup mozzarella, grated

¾ cup provolone, grated

2 teaspoons fresh parsley, chopped

Preheat the oven to 500°F.

Make white sauce.

If raw crust has contracted in the pan, stretch it back out. Spread 1 cup white sauce over the crust, leaving a ¼-inch border of uncovered dough. Dot the crust evenly with 1-inch dollops of ricotta. Sprinkle with oregano. Scatter mozzarella and provolone over the top.

Cook as directed in recipe for Pizza Margherita, sprinkling the pizza with parsley when it comes out of the oven.

Focaccia

MAKES 1 LARGE OR 2 SMALL FOCACCIA

Pronounced "fo-KAH-chee-ah," this soft, oily, crusty bread has been around since ancient Roman times. The basic version, given here, is seasoned with olive oil and salt, but you can add herbs such as rosemary, cheese such as Parmigiano-Reggiano, and veggies such as onion or tomato. Usually served as a side, focaccia also makes good sandwich bread and works as a thick pizza crust. "Dotting" the dough before baking, creating dents all over with your fingers, is part of the fun of making focaccia. This is a by-hand recipe, but you can also use a standing kitchen mixer or food processor.

....

1½ cups warm (100°F–110°F) water, plus more if needed.

1 packet (2¼ teaspoons) active dry yeast

2 tablespoons sugar

4 cups all-purpose flour, plus more for adjusting recipe and dusting work surface

1 tablespoon coarse sea salt, plus more for sprinkling

½–¾ cup extra-virgin olive oil, plus more for greasing bowl and brushing loaf

....

Before you start mixing, make sure water is correct temperature: Too cool or too warm, and yeast won't work.

In a medium mixing bowl, thoroughly combine water, yeast, and sugar. Let sit in a warm place for about 15 minutes. If it doesn't get bubbly, yeast is not working and you must discard mixture and start over again.

In a large mixing bowl, combine flour with salt. Pour in ¼ cup oil and slowly add yeast mixture, mixing with a large wooden spoon until the dough forms a soft, smooth ball. If dough is too dry while you're working it, add a little more water; if it is too wet, add a bit more flour.

Place dough on a lightly floured work surface. Knead once or twice—no more than that—and re-form into a ball. If the dough is sticky, sprinkle with a little more flour. Handle the dough as little as possible so it doesn't get tough.

Lightly grease another large mixing bowl with oil and add the dough. Roll the ball around to cover it with oil. Cover bowl loosely with plastic wrap or a clean kitchen towel. Put bowl in a warm spot until the dough doubles in size, about 1½ hours.

If you're making one large focaccia, grease a 13-x-18-inch baking sheet with ¼ cup oil; if you're making two smaller loaves, do the same to a second sheet. Punch down the dough in the bowl once or twice and place the entire ball on one pan, or divide it in half and put each piece on a separate pan.

Use your hands—not a rolling pin—to press and stretch the dough into a flattened oblong about ½ inch thick. It will probably cover about half the pan. Flip it over once or twice as you stretch to coat both sides with oil. Once you have formed the oblong, use your fingers to push holes into it, about 1 inch apart, all over the top. Cover the loaf with plastic wrap, and let it rest in a warm place until it puffs up, about 35 minutes.

While the dough is rising the second time, move racks to the two lowest rungs in the oven and preheat to 425°F.

When dough has risen, brush surface with more olive oil and sprinkle liberally with salt. If cooking one focaccia, slide pan onto lowest oven rack. If cooking two loaves on two pans, place one pan on each oven rack. Bake 20 to 25 minutes. If using two pans, switch them between shelves every 6 to 7 minutes, opening the oven door as briefly as possible. When the focaccia is golden brown on top, remove from the oven. Let cool before cutting.

Garlic Bread

SERVES 6–8

This decadent treat is a frequent side at many an Italian-American table. Buttery, toasty, and garlicky: What's not to like? You can use it as a pizza base if you like, but the simple addition of some cheese — nothing more — will bring forth oohs and aahs enough.

8 tablespoons (1 stick) salted butter
8 garlic cloves, crushed or minced
1 (16–18-inch) loaf Italian bread sliced horizontally into top and bottom
2 tablespoons fresh parsley, chopped

Preheat the oven to 350°F.

In a small saucepan, melt butter over medium-low heat. Add garlic and reduce heat to low. Let butter and garlic heat without bubbling for 5 minutes, stirring occasionally.

Lay two pieces of bread, cut side up, on a broiler pan. Brush very generously with the garlic butter, and spoon bits of garlic over the bread, spreading out evenly. Put pan into the oven and heat until bread starts to crisp, about 7 minutes. Remove pan from oven.

Turn oven to broil. When broiler is hot, slide in pan and toast bread until golden brown, about 2 minutes. Watch carefully so it doesn't burn. Remove bread from the broiler and sprinkle with parsley. Cut each half into 4 chunks and serve immediately.

VARIATION: CHEESY GARLIC BREAD

....

1 cup shredded mozzarella
1 cup shredded provolone
½ cup freshly grated Parmigiano-Reggiano or Pecorino Romano

....

Prepare garlic bread. Reduce oven temperature to 350°F.

In a medium mixing bowl, thoroughly combine cheeses. Pile cheese mixture onto the bread and put pan in oven. Cook until cheese just starts to melt. Remove bread from oven and turn oven to broil.

When broiler is hot, slide pan of bread onto lowest rung under the broiler, and toast until cheese is bubbling with golden brown patches on top. Watch carefully so it doesn't burn. Remove bread from broiler and sprinkle with parsley. Let cool for 2 minutes, cut each half into 4 chunks, and serve immediately.

CHAPTER FIVE

Vegetables and Sides

Italians love their vegetables so much that they have a whole category of dishes, *contorni* (singular *contorno*), which consists of nothing but vegetable side dishes. Their vegetable cookery doesn't stop there, however—far from it. Vegetables, herbs, grain, fruit, and nuts play a leading role throughout the meal, with olive oil the undisputed superstar. In every course, from the antipasto through the secondo, vegetables shine: in sautéed, baked, grilled, roasted, stewed, steamed, raw, pickled, marinated, and brined forms; served on their own or atop bread, pasta, fish, or meat; and transformed into sauces that appear across the menu. It's not surprising, because just about every kind of vegetable grows energetically in Italy's rich soil and mild climate.

Dozens of vegetables and herbs are native to Italy and the Mediterranean region, where they have been used since before the rise of the Roman Empire. Among those are artichokes, asparagus, bay, cabbage, celery, various mushrooms, lettuce, olives, oregano, parsley, rosemary, sage, and thyme. Over the millennia, numerous others were enthusiastically adopted from other parts of the world as well: basil, beans, bell and hot peppers, cacao, coffee, corn, eggplant, garlic, all kinds of greens, potatoes, rice, tomatoes, zucchini, and many more.

The world's first cookbook was Italian, published in the fourth or fifth century, and since then Italian cookbooks have highlighted vegetables. *Il Cuoco Galante* ("The Courteous Cook"), published in 1773 by Vincenzo Corrados of Naples, recommended a vegetarian diet of "fresh herbs, roots, flowers, fruits, seeds, and all that is produced in the earth for our nourishment. . . . There is no doubt that this kind of food appears to be more natural to man, and the use of meat is noxious." Even if you're a hardcore carnivore, you won't be able to resist Italian vegetable dishes, which are designed to intensify flavors and complement fish, poultry, and meat. Try some of these recipes and you'll be hooked.

Stuffed Artichokes

SERVES 4

One of the most classic of all Italian vegetables, artichokes are a central ingredient in countless Italian and Italian-American recipes. This version of stuffed artichokes leans toward the Italian-American, more generously and elaborately filled with bread crumbs and cheese. Never eaten an artichoke? Just pull off one leaf at a time, pile a little stuffing on it, and pull it through your teeth from top to bottom to scrape off the tender flesh along with the crumbs. When you reach the center, scrape out any fuzzy bits (the inedible, aptly named "choke"), and eat the heart with a fork and knife.

....

4 large artichokes

2 cups unseasoned bread crumbs

½ cup freshly grated Parmigiano-Reggiano or Pecorino Romano

½ cup fresh Italian (flat leaf) parsley, chopped

2 garlic cloves, minced

1 teaspoon lemon zest

Pinch of dried red pepper flakes

½ teaspoon salt

½ cup extra-virgin olive oil, plus more for finishing

1 lemon, quartered

....

With a large, sharp knife, cut off stems and top third of artichokes' globes. Pull off first couple of layers of tough leaves and discard.

Hold artichokes globe up under a strong stream of cold, running water, allowing the water to lift out any debris from between the leaves. Rinse the outside and put the artichokes upside down in a steamer basket in a large stock pot with about 1½ inches of water. Cover the pot and bring water to a boil over high heat; then reduce heat to medium-low. Simmer to steam the artichokes until their bases are tender, 30 to 35 minutes. If the water boils down too far, add more so artichokes continue to steam and the pot doesn't burn.

continued ▶

Remove artichokes from the pot, set them upside down on some paper towels, and allow to drain and cool. When cool, use your fingers to gently part the leaves at the center of the globes. Insert a grapefruit knife or spoon or a regular teaspoon, and scrape out the innermost small leaves, which curl inward and have prickly tips. Once you have removed those, dig out the fuzzy centers of the hearts; don't leave any of the choke fibers behind, but don't push out the bottoms of the hearts. Set the artichokes aside.

Preheat the oven to 375°F. In a medium mixing bowl, combine crumbs, cheese, parsley, garlic, lemon zest, pepper flakes, and salt. Toss well, then mix in oil.

Place artichokes, leaves up, on a work surface. Stuff centers with the crumb mixture. Part the surrounding leaves and pack the crumb mixture into spaces between the leaves.

Fit artichokes into a baking dish that will hold all 4 snugly. Bake until filling is golden brown and crusty, about 20 minutes. Remove dish from the oven and drizzle the artichokes with oil. Serve each with a wedge of lemon for squeezing over the top.

Asparagus Grilled in Prosciutto

SERVES 4

The sweet asparagus, lush prosciutto, and char from the grill make this simple dish a perfect delight. It's excellent next to grilled fish or chicken, making it an ideal summer treat. Serve it with some hollandaise for an extra treat.

16 fat asparagus spears, woody ends snapped off
2 tablespoons extra-virgin olive oil, plus more for finishing
1 teaspoon kosher salt
8 slices prosciutto
Toothpicks

Preheat the grill or broiler to hot.

In a large, covered saucepan over medium heat, steam asparagus until bright green and just tender—not soft. Remove asparagus to a large mixing bowl filled with ice water and cool to room temperature. Dry the asparagus and put on a small platter or in a medium baking dish or pan, drizzle with oil, and sprinkle with salt. Toss asparagus to coat.

On a clean work surface, lay out one slice of prosciutto. Center two spears of asparagus across one end of the slice. Roll up bundle and secure outer end of the prosciutto with a toothpick.

Place bundles on the grill rack crosswise to the wires to prevent bundles from falling into the fire. If broiling, slide broiler pan onto the middle rung of the broiler. Grill or broil the bundles, turning to cook them evenly and on all sides, until asparagus develops some charring. Do not char or dry out the prosciutto. Drizzle with olive oil and serve.

Tuscan Beans

SERVES 6–8

Since before anyone can remember, fellow Italians have joked that the Tuscans are mangiafagioli, or "bean-eaters." The name pokes fun at the legendary frugality of Tuscan cooks, who favor inexpensive ingredients prepared simply. With a gratifying dish like this one, though, the Tuscans get the last laugh. If you want to add a little more flavor to the recipe, toss in ¼ cup of diced pancetta or bacon before cooking. You can also prepare this in a slow cooker.

1 pound dried cannellini beans, debris picked out, rinsed, and drained

6 garlic cloves

2 fresh sage sprigs (6 leaves)

1 tablespoon coarse sea salt, plus more if needed

2 tablespoons extra-virgin olive oil

In a heavy saucepan or Dutch oven over medium-low heat, combine beans, garlic cloves, sage sprigs, and salt with 10 cups water. Cover and slowly bring beans to a simmer, about 1 hour. Cook the beans, stirring occasionally, until tender but not mushy, about 1 hour.

Remove pot from heat and let cool, covered, for about 20 minutes. Drain, remove garlic and sage, and season with salt. Drizzle with olive oil and serve.

Cauliflower Gratin

SERVES 4-6

*This comforting dish pairs especially well with grilled or roasted meats. Gratin
(what Americans call au gratin) originated in France, but the Italians long ago
embraced the cooking method as their own and use it for all kinds of vegetables.*

1 medium head cauliflower (about 2 pounds), leaves and stem removed and head
     cut into 1-inch pieces and florets
3 tablespoons unsalted butter
Salt and freshly ground black pepper

To prepare the cauliflower:

Put cauliflower in a steamer basket in a large saucepan filled with about 1½ inches
of water. Cover pot and bring water to a boil. Reduce heat to medium and steam
cauliflower until crisp but somewhat tender (not soft), about 5 minutes.

Drain well and allow to cool in the colander. Season cauliflower with salt and pepper. Grease a 9-x-13-inch baking dish with 1 tablespoon butter and add cauliflower.

Prepare the béchamel sauce.

To make the béchamel sauce:
4 tablespoons unsalted butter
4 tablespoons all-purpose flour
2 cups milk, heated to steaming
Salt
2 egg yolks
¾ cup freshly grated Parmigiano-Reggiano

continued ▶

In a medium saucepan over low heat, melt butter and stir in flour with a wooden spoon. Cook for 2 to 3 minutes, stirring constantly, until ingredients are thoroughly integrated. Do not allow the mixture to darken.

Remove from heat and slowly whisk in milk, pouring it in a thin, steady stream. Whisk until smooth and season with salt. Return pot to the stove and cook over low heat, stirring constantly, until the sauce thickens; it should feel like condensed cream.

Remove from heat. In a small mixing bowl, whisk egg yolks. When they are thoroughly whisked, continue whisking while slowly adding ¼ cup sauce to the bowl. Do not allow yolks to congeal. Once yolks are heated, slowly add them back into the sauce while whisking the sauce to blend thoroughly. Stir in ½ cup cheese.

To assemble the gratin:

Preheat the oven to 375°F.

Immediately pour béchamel evenly over cauliflower. Scatter remaining ¼ cup of cheese across the top and dot with remaining 2 tablespoons of butter.

Bake until top bubbles and browns lightly, about 25 minutes.

Spicy Sautéed Broccoli Rabe

SERVES 4

As green as green can be, leafy broccoli rabe (pronounced "rob") has a more intense flavor than broccoli and is slightly bitter. You may not be familiar with it, but it's readily available in supermarkets. Broccoli rabe is perfect when simply sautéed in olive oil to accompany meat or poultry dishes, mixed into pasta dishes, or added to panini.

3 tablespoons olive oil
4 garlic cloves, finely chopped
1 bunch (about 1 pound) broccoli rabe, cut into florets and 1-inch stem segments
⅛–¼ teaspoon red pepper flakes
Salt

In a large skillet over medium-low heat, heat oil with the garlic. When garlic starts to sizzle—don't let it brown—increase heat to medium and add broccoli rabe and pepper flakes (more or less according to taste) and season with salt. Toss thoroughly and sauté until rabe is bright green, about 3 minutes. Add ¼ cup water and cover skillet.

Simmer, stirring occasionally, until rabe is tender but not mushy, about 10 minutes. If the pan dries up while simmering, add a few more tablespoons water. When rabe is tender, uncover skillet and continue to simmer until water evaporates, about 5 minutes.

Eggplant Parmigiana

SERVES 8

Ahh, the joys of oozing red sauce, bubbling cheese, and creamy eggplant. Eggplant parmigiana is one of the classics of the Italian-American culinary canon, beloved of almost everyone who's dined on a red-checked tablecloth. Soothing in winter, delightful on a hero roll, and a sneaky way to get your kids to eat their vegetables, this is a dish that embodies the pampering warmth of an Italian nonna.

3 medium eggplants, peeled and cut lengthwise into ¼-inch-thick slices
Salt
1½ cups all-purpose flour
4 eggs, beaten
4 cups Italian-style seasoned bread crumbs
1 cup canola, peanut, or vegetable oil, plus more if needed
3½ cups pomodoro or marinara sauce (see page 2)
1 pound low-moisture mozzarella, shredded
1 cup freshly grated Parmigiano-Reggiano

Cover two baking sheets with a double layer of paper towels. Lay eggplant slices on paper towels in a single layer. Sprinkle with salt and set aside for 1 hour. The eggplant will lose some of its moisture so that finished casserole is not watery. After 1 hour, rinse eggplant slices, pat dry, and pile on a clean plate. Dry baking sheets and keep them handy.

Preheat the oven to 350°F.

Spread flour on a plate. Put beaten eggs into a wide, shallow bowl. Spread bread crumbs on a plate, about 1 cup at a time, while you work. One at a time, lightly flour eggplant slices on each side; then dip in the egg to coat, and generously cover each side with bread crumbs. Place coated slices in a single layer on baking sheets. In a large skillet, heat oil over medium-high heat until very hot but not smoking. Cover a large plate with a double layer of paper towels. When oil is hot, lay eggplant slices in the skillet in batches so that pieces are not touching. Fry until golden brown, turning over to fry both sides evenly. Remove to plate to drain. Put a layer of paper towels between the layers of eggplant as you stack them after cooking. Allow the oil to reheat between each batch of eggplant, adding more oil if needed.

In a 9-×-13-inch baking dish, spread enough sauce to coat in a ¼-inch-deep layer. Arrange a single layer of eggplant on top of the sauce. Sprinkle with cheeses. Spoon a coating of sauce over the top, and continue the process until all of the eggplant is in the pan. Top with a layer of sauce and finish with a layer of cheese.

Bake until the top is golden brown, 25 to 30 minutes.

Escarole with White Beans and Tomatoes

SERVES 4

This savory side is an excellent accompaniment to swordfish, chicken, or veal. If you prefer, pour it over a bowl of pasta to make a main course.

....

3 tablespoons olive oil

3 or 4 garlic cloves, minced

One head escarole, cut into 1-inch-wide strips

One 15-ounce can cannellini beans (or navy beans if you can't find cannellini), drained

One (14½-ounce) can diced tomatoes, with juice

Salt

Freshly grated Parmigiano-Reggiano or Pecorino Romano cheese, for sprinkling

....

Heat a large sauté pan or skillet over medium heat, and add oil and garlic. Heat until garlic just starts to sizzle—do not brown. Add escarole to the pan and sauté, stirring frequently, until the leaves are limp, about 5 minutes.

Put beans and tomatoes into the pan and mix well. Season with salt, cover pan, and simmer about 10 minutes to let the flavors combine.

Remove the lid, increase heat to medium-high, and cook for about 5 minutes to reduce the liquid by half. Serve with grated cheese on the side.

Green Beans and Tomatoes

SERVES 6-8

Fresh, young green beans are at their very best in summer, and if you can get them locally grown, this dish will shine with sweet flavor and light crispness—but it's lovely any time of year! Be sure to salt the water in which you boil the beans so they stay a nice, bright green. If you like, spice up this dish with a pinch or two of red pepper flakes.

....

1 tablespoon salt, plus more if needed

1 pound green beans, trimmed and snapped in half

3 tablespoons olive oil

2 medium shallots, finely chopped

2 cloves garlic, minced

1 (14½-ounce) can diced tomatoes, with juice

Freshly ground black pepper

Freshly grated Parmigiano-Reggiano or Pecorino Romano, for sprinkling

....

In a large saucepan over high heat, bring 1 gallon of water to a boil and add 1 tablespoon salt. Cook green beans until crisp but tender, drain, and run cold water over them to bring to room temperature. Drain well.

In a large skillet over medium heat, heat oil and add shallots and garlic. Cook until shallots are soft, about 3 minutes. Add tomatoes, increase heat to medium-high and bring sauce to a boil, then reduce heat to medium-low. Simmer until sauce thickens slightly, 15 to 20 minutes.

Add beans, stir well, and continue simmering until beans are tender, about 10 minutes. Season with salt and pepper, and serve with cheese on the side.

Potato Pie

SERVES 6

Italians love their mashed potatoes just as much as Americans do, and turn them into fantastic dishes like this one. An impressive yet easy side dish, potato pie also works well as an antipasto or brunch course.

2 pounds Yukon gold (waxy yellow) potatoes, peeled and cut into quarters
Salt
4 tablespoons unsalted butter, plus more for pan
¼ cup milk
2 eggs, beaten
1 cup freshly grated Parmigiano-Reggiano or Pecorino Romano, divided
Freshly ground black pepper
1 cup unseasoned bread crumbs
Extra-virgin olive oil, for drizzling

Put potatoes in a medium saucepan with enough water to cover them, plus ½ inch more. Add ½ teaspoon salt and bring water to a boil. Reduce heat to medium, and cook potatoes until tender, about 20 minutes. Drain well.

Preheat the oven to 350°F.

While potatoes are still hot, put in a bowl. Mash while adding butter, milk, and eggs. When butter is melted and mash is smooth, mix in ¾ cup cheese. Season with salt and pepper.

Grease a 9-inch cake pan or pie tin with butter. Coat bottom and sides with ½ cup of the bread crumbs. Spoon in potatoes and spread out evenly and smoothly to the edge of the pan. Sprinkle remaining bread crumbs and cheese over the top, and drizzle with olive oil.

Bake until topping browns and the potatoes are softly set. Remove the pan to a rack, and let cool for about 10 minutes. Slide a knife around the edge of the pan to loosen the pie from the pan. Cut into wedges to serve.

Roasted Potatoes

SERVES 6

You might not think of Italy as potato country, but in fact the average Italian eats almost one fourth the quantity of potatoes consumed by the average American. Italians have created some spectacular potato dishes, so their cookbook has a lot to offer this steak-and-spuds-crazy nation. Here is a distinctly Italian spin on roasted potatoes.

....

2½ pounds new (waxy red) potatoes, cut into ½-inch cubes

6 tablespoons extra-virgin olive oil

1 tablespoon kosher or coarse sea salt

6 garlic cloves, finely chopped

1 tablespoon fresh rosemary, minced, or 1 teaspoon dried and crumbled between your palms

1 tablespoon fresh oregano, minced, or 1 teaspoon dried and crumbled between your palms

....

Move oven racks to top and second-lowest rungs. Preheat the oven to 425°F.

In a large mixing bowl, toss together potatoes, oil, salt, garlic, and herbs. Transfer half the mixture to each of two large baking sheets, and distribute the pieces evenly across pans.

Bake, stirring occasionally and switching pans halfway through, until potatoes are tender inside and brown and crispy outside, 30 to 40 minutes.

Grilled Radicchio and Romaine

SERVES 4

Grilled lettuce, you say? Yes! Italian cuisine includes numerous recipes that use cooked lettuce, and this one makes the most of that favorite Italian cooking method, grilling. The leaves develop an appealing char on the outside but remain crisp but tender on the inside. This is an absolutely superb warm-weather dish that complements grilled fish, poultry, and meat alike.

....

1 cup everyday balsamic vinegar

2 large hearts of romaine, or 2 heads with the outermost 2 or 3 layers of leaves removed

2 large heads of red treviso (long) radicchio, cut in half lengthwise, or 2 large heads of red round radicchio, quartered

½ cup extra-virgin olive oil

Coarse sea salt

8 ounces young goat cheese, crumbled or cut into small (¼-inch) chunks

....

In a small saucepan over medium-high heat, bring vinegar to a boil. Lower heat to medium and reduce the vinegar, stirring regularly. When it starts to thicken, begin stirring constantly. In about 20 minutes the vinegar will be half its original volume and thicken to the consistency of olive oil. It should leave a coating on a teaspoon dipped into it. Remove from heat and set aside.

Preheat grill to high.

Cut romaine in half lengthwise, leaving the base intact to hold the leaves together. Quarter the radicchio top to bottom, also leaving the base intact.

Put lettuces into a large baking pan, pour the oil over them, and sprinkle liberally with salt. Gently tumble the lettuces to coat with the oil and salt, without breaking leaves off of the segments.

Put the lettuces on the grill rack directly over the fire, placing the segments perpendicular to the wires so they don't fall through. Grill lettuces, turning segments regularly to cook all sides evenly, until outsides are moderately charred but not burned.

Remove lettuces to a serving platter. Scatter cheese across the top and drizzle with a few tablespoons of vinegar.

Spinach with Pignoli, Raisins, and Anchovies

SERVES 6

Dark leafy greens, prepared in innumerable ways, are rarely missing from an Italian meal, and spinach is no exception. When buying spinach for this recipe, bypass the bags and boxes of fragile, mild baby variety in favor of bunches of mature leaves packed with spinach flavor. You can leave out the anchovy if you prefer, but it lends a touch of saltiness that makes this dish pop.

....

6 tablespoons extra-virgin olive oil, divided

4 large garlic cloves, finely chopped

2 flat anchovy filets, chopped

2 pounds fresh spinach, de-stemmed and torn into rough pieces

½ teaspoon salt

½ cup golden raisins

½ cup toasted pignoli (pine nuts)

....

In a large skillet over medium heat, heat 4 tablespoons of oil, garlic, and anchovies. Mash anchovies with the back of a spoon until they form a paste.

Add spinach in clumps, letting the leaves wilt to make room for the next clump, until all spinach is in pan. Add salt and raisins, mix thoroughly, cover pan, and cook for 5 minutes, stirring occasionally.

Remove cover and continue cooking until liquid evaporates from pan. Toss in the pignoli, adjust seasoning, add the remaining 2 tablespoons of oil, and cook for 2 or 3 more minutes.

Zucchini Ripieni

SERVES 4

These individual stuffed zucchini make a charming accompaniment to poultry or veal dishes. If you're looking for a way to cook a monster zucchini from your garden, make the same filling and bake twice as long.

4 small zucchini, cut in half lengthwise

2 tablespoons extra-virgin olive oil, plus more for finishing

1 small onion, finely chopped

4 garlic cloves, finely chopped

¼ cup white or cremini mushrooms, chopped

2 medium tomatoes, seeded and chopped

Salt and freshly ground black pepper

½ cup unseasoned bread crumbs

¼ cup Italian (flat leaf) parsley, chopped, or 1 tablespoon dried

1 teaspoon fresh thyme, chopped, or ½ teaspoon dried

1 teaspoon fresh oregano, chopped, or ¼ teaspoon dried

¾ cup freshly grated Parmigiano-Reggiano

2 tablespoons softened butter

1 egg, beaten

Preheat the oven to 375°F.

Using a spoon, scoop seeds out of the zucchini halves to make 8 little boats. Leave about ½ inch of flesh on inside walls of the boats. Chop removed flesh and set aside.

In a large skillet over medium-high heat, heat oil and sauté onion and garlic until onion turns transparent, about 4 minutes. Add mushrooms and cook for 2 minutes, stirring occasionally. Add chopped zucchini and tomatoes, season with salt and pepper, and sauté for 2 minutes. Remove pan from the heat.

continued ▶

In a medium mixing bowl, combine the bread crumbs, parsley, thyme, oregano, and cheese. Season with salt and pepper. Transfer vegetables from the pan to the bowl, and mix in the butter and egg.

Spoon the stuffing into the zucchini boats. If there is excess stuffing, mound it on top and pat it down slightly. Place the zucchini in a baking dish and drizzle with olive oil. Bake until the stuffing is golden brown on top and the zucchini boats are fork tender, about 30 minutes.

Creamy Polenta with Mushrooms

SERVES 4

Cornmeal is cooked into a wide variety of dishes around the world: shrimp and grits in the southern United States; tamales in Mexico; all kinds of breads and porridges in Europe, Africa, Asia, and the Americas; and polenta in Italy. When compared with the versions in other countries, cooked Italian polenta has a lighter, creamier texture because even the medium-grain variety sold in Italy is somewhat finer than ground cornmeal sold elsewhere. Be sure to buy an Italian brand, either in your supermarket or online. Don't use "instant" polenta if you want a smooth texture. Like the finished dish itself, the cornmeal used to make it is called polenta.

....

5 cups whole or low-fat milk

1 cup dry medium-grain Italian polenta (yellow or white)

¼ cup freshly grated Parmigiano-Reggiano

Salt and freshly ground black pepper

3 tablespoons extra-virgin olive oil

1 garlic clove, minced

½ pound shiitake mushrooms, soil brushed off, stems removed, cut into thin slices

½ pound white or cremini mushrooms, soil brushed off, stems removed, cut into thin slices

2 tablespoons fresh Italian (flat leaf) parsley, finely chopped

1 teaspoon fresh thyme, chopped, or ½ teaspoon dried

½ cup Madeira, dry sherry (not cooking sherry), dry vermouth, or rich chicken stock

3 tablespoons cold unsalted butter

....

In a medium saucepan over medium heat, bring milk to a boil, stirring slowly and constantly. When boiling, start whisking and slowly add the polenta in a thin, steady stream. Keep milk at a boil and don't stop whisking until all polenta is combined with the milk. Reduce heat to low and stir the polenta with a wooden spoon for 2 minutes. Cover pot and cook for 10 minutes.

Uncover, stir for 1 minute, cover, and repeat five times until an hour has elapsed. Give the polenta a last 1-minute stir before removing from the heat.

continued ▶

Stir in the cheese and season with salt and pepper. Cover, and be ready to use it immediately.

While the polenta is cooking, heat the oil in a medium skillet over medium-high heat. Add the garlic and mushrooms and sauté, stirring occasionally, until mushrooms are tender, about 8 minutes.

Add herbs and the wine or stock. Cook, scraping any brown bits off bottom of the pan, until the liquid reduces by half. Season with salt and pepper. Melt the cold butter into the sauce and stir well.

As soon as the polenta is cooked, spoon into shallow bowls and top with mushrooms. Serve while hot.

Polenta Triangles with Creamy Gorgonzola Sauce

SERVES 4

When cooked polenta cools, it sets into a firm, sliceable form. This takes several hours, so after the polenta reaches room temperature, you may want to put it in the refrigerator overnight, sealed tightly in plastic wrap. The nutty, crispy polenta in this recipe is an ideal base for the velvety, tangy gorgonzola sauce.

1 batch cooked polenta, prepared according to the Creamy Polenta with
    Mushrooms recipe, omitting the Parmigiano-Reggiano
1 tablespoon unsalted butter
3 tablespoons fresh parsley, minced, for garnish
½ cup walnuts, toasted and broken into ¼-inch pieces (optional)

When the polenta finishes cooking, immediately pour it into a 9-×-11-inch baking dish that has been greased with butter. Smooth out to an even depth and allow to cool to room temperature. Press plastic wrap directly onto the surface to cover. Refrigerate at least 2 hours, or as long as overnight.

To make the gorgonzola sauce:
2 cups heavy cream
2 cups whole or low-fat milk
5 ounces regular gorgonzola cheese (not the dolce variety)
Salt and freshly ground black pepper
½ cup olive oil

In a medium saucepan over medium-high heat, bring cream and milk to a boil. Boil, stirring occasionally, until mixture thickens, about 45 minutes.

continued ▶

Remove from heat and whisk in cheese until it melts. Season with salt and pepper. Cover and keep warm until polenta triangles are ready.

To prepare triangles:

Run a knife around the edge of the dish of cooled polenta to separate it from the walls. Place a clean cutting board (large enough to cover the entire dish) on top of the baking dish. Quickly flip the board and dish over together so polenta comes out of the dish and onto the board in one piece. Cut the rectangle of polenta in half lengthwise and then crosswise. Cut each square diagonally into two triangles.

Preheat the oven to 250°F.

In a large skillet, heat oil over medium-high until very hot but not smoking. Cover a baking sheet with a layer of paper towels. When the oil is hot, lay 4 polenta triangles in the skillet so that they are not touching. Fry until golden brown and crisp on each side, about 8 minutes per side.

Remove to the baking sheet to drain, placing pan in the oven to keep warm. Allow the oil to reheat; then fry the second batch of polenta. Lay paper towels over the first batch of triangles in the oven, remove the second batch from the pan, and place on paper towels to drain.

Arrange 2 polenta triangles on each of 4 plates. Whisk the warm gorgonzola sauce for 1 minute; then spoon the sauce over the triangles. Garnish with parsley and walnuts (if using) and serve while hot.

CHAPTER SIX

Pasta and Risotto

For many people, nothing says "Italy" louder and clearer than pasta. It's true that pasta occupies a very special place in Italian cuisine. No other single food—not pizza, not tomatoes, not salami, not veal—claims its very own, exclusive course on the menu. In an Italian meal the pasta course is called *primi,* meaning "first," and in the hearts of Italians, pasta is undoubtedly the first of all ingredients. Pasta may be the country's only truly universal food, an integral part of every region's cuisine.

Per capita, Italians eat roughly three times as much pasta as Americans. They eat it not only as a *primi* but as a meal all its own, whether a light lunch or a hearty dinner (with no *secondi,* or meat course). Beyond the classic pasta-on-a-plate-with-sauce renditions, pasta can be served hot or cold, in soups or casseroles, as a snack, or even in breakfast or dessert dishes. In Italy, pasta is everywhere and has been for a long, long time.

It's possible that the kind of pasta eaten today originated in twelfth-century Sicily, a century and a half before Venetian explorer Marco Polo brought noodles back with him from China—if in fact he did so (a lot of experts doubt it). Fresh pasta, made at home from soft flour and eggs and eaten on the spot, developed early on and was eaten by all classes of Italians. Dried pasta, made of hard—and hard-to-work-with—durum wheat was a rarity, eaten only by the privileged. That changed during the industrial revolution of the late nineteenth century, when machines took over the labor-intensive job of making dried pasta, and its price plummeted. Since then, dry pasta has become king: a cheap, filling, easy-to-cook, readily transportable food with a long shelf life.

All that, and tasty to boot! With so many styles and shapes to choose from, pasta is one of Italy's most versatile ingredients. It can be prepared to suit any season, occasion, or palate, matched with just about any other ingredients imaginable. That's just what Italians have done, with the same vast regional variations reflected in their vegetable, meat, and seafood dishes. In the north, white sauces and butter are favored above tomato-based sauces, and fresh pasta predominates. To the south, more tomatoes, garlic, herbs, olives, and vegetables come into play, and on the islands and in coastal regions, pasta is often paired with seafood. Even the name of different pasta shapes changes from place to place: What we call cavatelli has twenty-eight different names across Italy.

But, as they say, it's all good.

Dried vs. Fresh Pasta

When buying pasta, you have a choice between *pasta secca* (dried) and *pasta fresca* (fresh). Unlike with vegetables or fish, fresh is not always best. Italian pasta dishes call for one or the other depending on the results the cook is looking for. Some pasta shapes come in both dried and fresh versions, giving you the flexibility to mix things up a little.

Dried Pasta: The typical American supermarket carries dozens of kinds of dried pasta, in many shapes and made from all kinds of ingredients. Classic dried pasta shapes include spaghetti, linguine, penne, and conchiglie (shells). The traditional form is made of semolina flour that comes from hard durum wheat, but you'll come across Italian-style pastas made with everything from whole wheat to rice and from Jerusalem artichokes to quinoa. The only other component of traditional dried pasta is water, but you can buy pasta that incorporates spinach, beets, carrots, lemon juice, ground black pepper, *sepia* (squid ink), or other ingredients. Only spinach adds any actual flavor, and squid ink produces an unpleasant texture, so most of these additives are pointless beyond their color. Bronze-cut pasta, made using an old-fashioned technique, sometimes on very old equipment, is generally imported from Italy. It offers the best dried-pasta experience because its rough texture soaks up sauce and feels great in your mouth. It's more expensive and a little harder to find, but it's 110 percent worth it.

Fresh Pasta: The silky texture and ethereal flavor of fresh pasta provides an entirely different eating experience than that of dried pasta. Most fresh pasta is made of soft, low-gluten (e.g., all-purpose or cake) flour and eggs, and is cut into flat ribbons of various widths, such as fettuccine, tagliatelle, and pappardelle. Fresh pasta can also be stuffed with cheese, vegetables, or meat to create ravioli, tortellini, and other filled shapes. Another kind of fresh pasta is made with semolina flour and water, just as dried pasta is, but is not completely dried before cooking. Orecchiette ("little ears") and farfalle (bow ties) are a couple of shapes that are made this way. As with dried pasta, extra ingredients such as vegetables and seasonings don't really add much to pure, yellow fresh pasta. You can make fresh pasta at home if you have the time and patience, but you can also find it in the refrigerator section of your supermarket. It will be partially or even completely dried, but that's okay. Fresh pasta, especially the stuffed shapes, is also sold frozen, but the frozen varieties, while convenient, don't have the same elegance.

Pasta Shapes

Italians have invented literally hundreds of shapes of pasta and have given those shapes just as many names. Both dried and fresh pasta take several forms, and many shapes come in both fresh and dried versions. Here's a guide to some of the shapes you're likely to encounter, divided up into categories.

Strands

- Capellini d'angelo ("angel hairs"): the thinnest of the strands
- Capellini ("fine hairs"): thicker than angel hair, thinner than vermicelli
- Fusilli lunghi ("long rifles"): long spring-shaped strands
- Spaghetti alla chitarra ("guitar spaghetti"): similar to spaghetti, except square
- Spaghetti ("twines"): most common strand pasta
- Spaghettini ("little twines"): thin spaghetti
- Vermicelli ("little worms"): thicker than capellini, thinner than spaghetti

Ribbons

- Fettuccine ("little ribbons"): ribbons about ⅜-inch wide
- Lasagne, singular: *lasagna* ("cooking pot"): very wide noodles, often with fluted edges
- Linguettine: narrower version of linguine
- Linguine ("little tongues"): about the width of spaghetti
- Pappardelle: 1-inch-wide ribbons

- Tagliatelle (from *tagliare*, "to cut"): narrower version of fettuccine
- Taglierini: narrower version of tagliatelle

Tubes

- Bucatini ("little holes"): thick, hollow spaghetti
- Cannelloni ("big pipes," "big reeds"): large tubes for stuffing
- Ditali ("thimbles"): small, short tubes
- Ditalini ("little thimbles"): smaller version of ditali
- Gomito maccheroni: elbow macaroni
- Garganelli: square egg noodles rolled into short tubes
- Maccheroni: straight version of gomito maccheroni, usually ridged
- Manicotti ("sleeves"): ridged cannelloni for stuffing
- Mostaccioli ("mustaches"): un-ridged version of penne
- Penne, penne rigate ("quills"): medium-length tubes with ridges, cut diagonally at both ends
- Rigatoni (from *riga*, "line"): large, slightly curved, ridged tubes
- Ziti ("little girls"): long, narrow, smooth tubes, usually broken into 2-inch pieces before cooking

Specialty Shapes

- Cavatelli (from *cavare*, "to hollow"): small circles rolled in on themselves to resemble cowrie shells
- Conchiglie ("small seashells"): resemble tiny conch shells
- Conchigliette ("little seashells"): smaller version of conchiglie
- Conchiglioni ("large seashells"): large, stuffable version of conchiglie
- Farfalle ("butterflies"): shaped like bow ties or butterflies
- Farfalline ("little butterflies"): smaller version of farfalle

- Fusilli (from *fucile*, "rifle" [the inside of a gun barrel is grooved like a screw]): short, flat ribbons twisted into a screw shape

- Gemelli ("twins"): flat *s*-shaped ribbons twisted to resemble two strands wrapped around each other, about 2 inches long

- Orecchiette ("little ears"): shaped like little bowls

- Radiatore ("radiators"): curls with deep, concentric, ruffled fins, modeled on a type of old radiator

- Rotelle ("little wheels"): shaped like wagon wheels

- Rotini ("twists"): corkscrew-shaped spirals similar to fusilli

- Spirali ("spirals"): short tubes twisted into spirals, resembles fusilli lunghi

- Spiralini ("little spirals"): more tightly-coiled spirali

- Strozzapreti ("priest stranglers"): flat squares rolled into short, tight cylinders

Tiny Shapes

- Anelli ("rings"): rings or "O's"

- Fregula: toasted little balls or beads, like large couscous

- Orzo ("barley"): shaped like large grains of rice

- Pastina ("little pasta"): miniscule spheres

- Quadrettini ("little squares"): small, flat squares

- Stelle ("stars"): miniature star shapes

- Stelline ("little stars"): smaller version of stelle

Filled Shapes

- Agnolotti ("priests' hats"): small square pockets

- Mezzelune ("half-moons"): semicircular pockets

- Ravioli (probably from *rava*, "turnip"): large square pockets

- Tortelli: rectangular version of ravioli, sometimes twisted at the end to resemble wrapped candy

- Tortellini (from *tortello*, "pie"): a semicircular pocket pinched together at the corners to form a ring

- Tortelloni (from *tortello*, "pie"): larger version of tortellini

Cooking Pasta

One of the biggest mistakes people make when cooking pasta is to use too small a pot and too little water. To cook 1 pound of pasta properly, you must use at least 4 quarts of water in a pot that will hold twice as much, otherwise the pasta will stick together and turn out gluey. If you're cooking less than that, even a very small amount, never use less than 3 quarts of water. If you're cooking more than a pound, add 2 more cups of water for an additional ¼ pound, a quart more for ½ pound, 6 more cups for ¾ pound, or two quarts for 1 pound. Never cook more than 2 pounds at a time, as the pasta will neither cook nor drain properly.

Another must for cooking pasta is to use water that is sufficiently hot. Before you put the pasta in the pot, the water should be boiling rapidly. Once the pasta is in, bring the water back up to a full boil as quickly as possible, and keep it boiling rapidly until the pasta is done. Cooking pasta at too low a temperature will make the noodles gummy.

To heighten pasta's flavor, add 1½ tablespoons of salt for every gallon of water once the water has come to a boil. The salt will reduce the water's temperature, so wait for the full boil to return before putting in the pasta.

Don't add oil to the cooking water. Contrary to what you might think, oil won't keep the noodles from sticking together. All it does is to coat them so that they don't absorb the water properly. You'll have to cook it longer, and you'll end up with slimy pasta.

When you add the pasta to the boiling water, put the entire batch in at once so that all of the pieces cook evenly. If strands are sticking out of the water when you put them in, push their tops down into the water with a long spoon, trying not to break the pieces. Whatever the pasta shape, stir it immediately when it goes into the water, and frequently throughout the cooking process, to keep it from sticking to itself or the pot.

The cooking time for pasta varies widely depending on its size and shape, so be sure to follow the cooking directions on the package. As a rule of thumb, fresh pasta takes about half as long to cook as similarly shaped dried pasta. Cook pasta to an *al dente* texture (literally, "to the tooth") so it is cooked through but still firm to bite, not soggy and flavorless. During the last minute or so of the cooking time indicated on the package, take a piece of pasta out of the pot every 20 seconds and bite it to test doneness. Drain the pasta when it's underdone; it will continue to cook for a few seconds after you drain it.

Drain pasta in a colander the instant it's done cooking, so it doesn't overcook. Don't rinse it, unless a recipe clearly instructs that you do so. Shake the colander to help all of the water to drain out. Sauce the pasta immediately, tossing thoroughly to coat every strand. If you aren't saucing, put the pasta into a bowl and toss it with a little olive oil right away—if un-sauced pasta sits in a colander or bowl for even a minute before saucing, it will stick together in a mass. Don't return un-sauced pasta to the empty cooking pot either, as it will stick to the sides and bottom. Have your sauce or toppings ready before the pasta is finished cooking, and serve the pasta immediately after you sauce it. Cooked pasta that sits around before you eat it will turn gloppy and sticky.

How much pasta to cook? Dried pasta usually doubles from its original size, so most recipes made with 1 pound of dried pasta will serve 6 to 8 people as a first course or side dish; 4 to 6 as a main course. Fresh pasta retains its original size, so you'll need about 1½ pounds to serve the same crowd.

Matching Sauces with Pastas

Although the following recipes call for a specific pasta shape, most of them work well with more than one type of pasta, so free to mix and match. If you choose to do so, you'll get the best results if you keep in mind a few guidelines. The firmer texture of dried pasta makes it a good match for bold flavors and hearty ingredients such as tomato sauce, garlic, seafood, and summer vegetables like eggplant and zucchini. Dried pasta also stands up in soup, stew, and baked dishes. By contrast, the delicate flavor and texture of fresh pasta shine brightest with butter- and cream-based sauces, herbs, and spring vegetables like asparagus and peas. Tubular pasta such as penne and specialty shapes such as rotelle are the best matches for chunky sauces, which integrate well with the shapes rather than sliding off of them. Tubes are also good for baked dishes, as are large, fillable shapes and large rectangular shapes that can be layered. Strands and ribbons are better for smoother tomato and cream sauces, as well as pesto and other olive oil-based sauces. They also work well in dishes that are topped with items such as meatballs or shrimp. But again, these are only guidelines: Follow your taste buds!

Arborio Rice

There would be no risotto without arborio. Well, there are other varieties of rice that make (arguably better) risotto—notably Carnaroli and Vialone Nano—but they're expensive and harder to find in the United States. Your supermarket most likely carries arborio, and while it's more expensive than "regular" rice, it can do things that Uncle Ben can only dream about. This strictly Italian stuff has a distinct personality: The short, plump grains contain a unique kind of starch that turns them creamy and chewy when cooked. Arborio picks up other flavors beautifully, so when cooked right risotto is a luxurious, delectable wonder.

A few things to keep in mind when cooking risotto: There's nothing complicated about making it, but it does require your undivided attention for 35 minutes or so, the time it takes to prepare only the rice portion of the dish. The technique is easy, but it differs from that used to cook other kinds of rice. *Do not rinse arborio rice before cooking!* Instead of putting all of the rice and all of the liquid in the pot simultaneously, covering the pot, and leaving it to cook on its own, you'll start the rice without liquid in the pot and gradually add the liquid over the course of the process. You'll keep the pot uncovered, and as the rice absorbs each infusion of liquid you'll add more, stirring constantly all the while. This action develops the starch in the rice, so the risotto turns creamy (other types of rice don't behave the same way). As the rice soaks up the liquid, just be sure the pot doesn't dry out entirely—if it does, your rice will stick to the pot and get crispy, ruining the creamy texture that you're after. Like pasta, risotto should be cooked until al dente: tender in the center, but still firm to bite.

Capellini with Fresh Tomatoes, Garlic, and Basil

SERVES 6–8 AS A FIRST COURSE OR SIDE DISH; 4–6 AS A MAIN COURSE

As simple and quick as it gets, this dish is best in late summer, when sweet tomatoes burst from the vine and aromatic basil grows in lavish clumps.

....

3 tablespoons extra-virgin olive oil
3 garlic cloves, minced
3 medium tomatoes, cored, seeded, and chopped
1 pound dried capellini, cooked al dente according to package directions
2 tablespoons fresh basil, chopped
Salt and freshly ground black pepper
Freshly grated Parmigiano-Reggiano or Pecorino Romano, for sprinkling

....

In a large skillet, heat olive oil over medium heat and add garlic. Cook until garlic starts to sizzle but doesn't brown, about 2 minutes. Add tomatoes to the pan and cook until they soften slightly, about 3 minutes.

Reduce heat to low and add capellini and basil. Toss well and season with salt and pepper; then cook, tossing, for 2 minutes. Serve with cheese on the side.

Farfalle alla Vodka

**SERVES 6-8 AS A FIRST COURSE OR SIDE DISH;
4-6 AS A MAIN COURSE**

This dish is a modern Italian invention that dates back only to the 1970s, but since then it has been wildly popular both in Italy and the United States. The vodka, added to intensify the tomato flavor, evaporates during cooking, so don't hesitate to serve this to the kids (they'll love it). Vodka sauce is usually served with penne, but whimsical farfalle play well with the pale pink sauce.

To make the vodka sauce:
1 tablespoon extra-virgin olive oil
1 tablespoon unsalted butter
1 small onion, minced
2 cloves garlic, minced
Pinch of red pepper flakes
One (28-ounce) can crushed tomatoes
½ cup vodka
¾ cup heavy cream
1 tablespoon fresh basil, chopped
Salt and freshly ground black pepper

In a medium saucepan over medium heat, melt butter into olive oil. Add onion and cook until lightly browned, about 5 minutes. Add garlic and red pepper and cook for 2 more minutes.

Stir in tomatoes and vodka. Bring sauce to a simmer and cook, stirring occasionally, until alcohol evaporates, 8 to 10 minutes.

Stir in cream and basil, season with salt and pepper, and cook just long enough to warm the sauce through.

To assemble the dish:

1 pound dried farfalle, cooked al dente according to package directions

When the farfalle is ready, transfer to a large bowl and pour in vodka sauce. Toss thoroughly and serve immediately.

Fettuccine Alfredo

**SERVES 4–6 AS A FIRST COURSE OR SIDE DISH;
2–4 AS A MAIN COURSE**

In 1914, a Roman restaurateur's pregnant wife lost her appetite. After trying one thing and another, the man—named Alfredo—finally came up with a dish she would eat. She loved it, and he began serving it in his Alfredo restaurants, both in Italy and the United States. A family secret until recently, the original Fettuccine Alfredo is much lighter than the gooey dish familiar to Americans, and much more delicious.

2 sticks unsalted butter, brought to room temperature and cut into
    teaspoon-size slices
1½ pounds fresh fettuccine, cooked al dente according to package directions,
    with ¾ cup cooking water reserved
3 cups freshly grated Parmigiano-Reggiano
Salt and freshly ground black pepper

In a 250°F oven, heat a large serving platter until warm. Remove platter from oven and place the butter on it. Put the fettuccini on top of the butter and sprinkle with cheese. Pour on ¼ cup hot cooking water.

With a large serving fork and spoon, toss pasta with the other ingredients. If necessary, add more pasta water to meld the butter and cheese into a smooth sauce. Continue tossing until fettuccine is thoroughly coated with sauce and there are no unmixed ingredients on the platter. Serve immediately with salt and pepper on the side.

Linguine with White Clam Sauce

**SERVES 6-8 AS A FIRST COURSE OR SIDE DISH;
4-6 AS A MAIN COURSE**

Most Italians would never make this dish with canned clams, but the pre-cleaned, pre-shucked variety in cans or jars (whole are far better than minced) are so much easier to handle that this adaptation will probably work better for you. One old Italian rule that you should stick by, however, is to never, ever serve grated cheese with clam sauce.

To make the white clam sauce:

3 (10-ounce) cans whole clams
4 tablespoons extra-virgin olive oil, plus more for finishing
6 garlic cloves, sliced
1 cup white wine
2 tablespoons fresh oregano, chopped, or 1 tablespoon dried
2 tablespoons fresh Italian (flat leaf) parsley, chopped
¼ teaspoon red pepper flakes

In a large strainer over a bowl, drain clams. Set liquid aside and allow any sand to settle to the bottom, about 15 minutes. Roughly chop clams into 2 or 3 pieces each. Set aside in a covered bowl.

In a large skillet, heat oil over medium heat and add garlic. Cook until garlic browns lightly, about 2 minutes. Add 1 cup clam juice and the wine, oregano, and parsley. Bring to a simmer and cook for 25 minutes.

Remove from heat and add red pepper and chopped clams. Stir well.

To assemble the dish:

1 pound dried linguine, cooked al dente according to package directions

continued ▶

When sauce is ready, add linguine to the pot and toss to coat. Serve immediately with a drizzle of oil on top.

VARIATION: RED CLAM SAUCE

Red clam sauce, an American spin on the Italian original, has become a staple at the Italian-American table. Follow the previous recipe, adding one 14½-ounce can of diced tomatoes, with the juice, to the skillet along with the clam juice and wine. Simmer for 35 minutes instead of 25, and increase the oregano, parsley, and red pepper if you like.

Orecchiette with Sausage and Broccoli Rabe

**SERVES 6–8 AS A FIRST COURSE OR SIDE DISH;
4–6 AS A MAIN COURSE**

The dark green bitterness of the broccoli rabe, the crumbly savoriness of the sausage, and the robust texture of the pasta make this a quintessential Italian dish.

1½ pounds hot Italian sausage
¼ cup extra-virgin olive oil
3 garlic cloves, minced
2 bunches broccoli rabe, de-stemmed and roughly chopped
½ cup white wine
Salt and freshly ground black pepper
1 pound dried orecchiette, cooked al dente according to package directions
½ cup freshly grated Parmigiano-Reggiano or Pecorino Romano, plus more
    for sprinkling

Slit sausage casings lengthwise and scrape stuffing into a small mixing bowl. Cover and set aside.

In a large skillet, heat oil with garlic over medium heat until garlic sizzles but does not brown. When pan is hot, add sausage meat and cook, stirring to break up clumps, until sausage browns, about 5 minutes. Add broccoli rabe and continue cooking until greens are crisp yet tender.

Pour in wine and deglaze the pan, scraping brown bits off the bottom. Simmer until the broccoli is fully tender, but not soft. Season with salt and pepper.

Add the orecchiette to the pan and toss to coat. Sprinkle cheese onto the pasta and toss until all ingredients are well-combined. Serve immediately with cheese on the side.

Penne Puttanesca

**SERVES 6–8 AS A FIRST COURSE OR SIDE DISH;
4–6 AS A MAIN COURSE**

*An ideal winter dish, but delicious any time of year, this quick, rich preparation
bursts with the essence of southern Italy. Its bold flavor inspired its name, which is a
tribute to ladies of the evening.*

To make the puttanesca sauce:
¼ cup olive oil
4 or 5 garlic cloves, chopped
1 (2-ounce) tin anchovy fillets, drained
½ teaspoon red pepper flakes
½ cup oil-cured or kalamata olives, pitted and chopped
3 tablespoons capers
1 (28-ounce) can crushed tomatoes
Salt and freshly ground pepper

Heat a large sauté pan or skillet over medium heat, and add olive oil, garlic, anchovies, and red pepper. Sauté, mashing anchovies with the back of a spoon, for about
5 minutes.

Stir in olives, capers, and tomatoes and bring to a simmer. Reduce heat slightly and
season with salt and pepper. Cook for 8–10 minutes.

To assemble the dish:
1 pound dried penne, cooked al dente according to package directions
Freshly grated Parmigiano-Reggiano or Pecorino Romano cheese, for sprinkling

When the penne is ready, pour into pan and stir thoroughly until completely coated
in sauce. Heat for about 2 minutes, and serve immediately with cheese on the side.

Rigatoni alla Napoletana

**SERVES 6-8 AS A FIRST COURSE OR SIDE DISH;
4-6 AS A MAIN COURSE**

This sauce, like the Bolognese sauce later in the chapter, is an example of the Italian sauces known as ragù, *which are meat sauces that often contain tomatoes. Here, meat is simply a flavoring for the sauce. If you're serving the rigatoni as a first course or side dish, reserve the meat for your* secondo *or another use; if the rigatoni will be your main course, you can shred or chop the meat to go on top of your sauced pasta.*

....

To make the *Ragù alla Napoletana*:

¼ cup extra-virgin olive oil

1-pound piece boneless beef rump, bottom round, chuck, or brisket

1-pound piece boneless pork shoulder, butt, or blade

1 tablespoon salt, plus more if needed

2 garlic cloves

1 medium onion, chopped

½ cup dry red wine

1 (28-ounce) can crushed tomatoes

Pinch of red pepper flakes (optional)

Freshly ground black pepper

....

In a large saucepan or Dutch oven, heat oil over medium-high heat until very hot but not smoking. Put both pieces of meat into pot, sprinkle with 1 tablespoon salt, and cook, turning occasionally until juices seep out and are browned on all sides, about 15 minutes.

Reduce heat to medium and add garlic and onion. Keep turning meat and cook until onion is golden, about 10 minutes.

Increase heat to medium-high and add wine, tomatoes, and red pepper (if using).

Bring liquid to a boil; then reduce heat to low and cover pot. Simmer, stirring occasionally and adding water if needed, until meat is very tender, at least 3 hours. The sauce should be thick enough to coat a spoon. Remove meat from the pot and season sauce with salt and pepper.

continued ▶

To assemble the dish:

1 pound dried rigatoni, cooked al dente according to package directions

Freshly grated Parmigiano-Reggiano or Pecorino Romano for sprinkling

When the rigatoni is ready, transfer to a large bowl and pour in the sauce. Toss thoroughly and serve immediately with cheese on the side.

Spaghetti alla Carbonara

**SERVES 6-8 AS A FIRST COURSE OR SIDE DISH;
4-6 AS A MAIN COURSE**

Breakfast for dinner or dinner for breakfast. How about brunch? You can have it any way with this Roman bacon-and-eggs pasta dish. A lot of American versions add onions and cream, but the authentic recipe yields sweet, creamy results on its own. Make sure your skillet's not too hot, or the eggs will scramble.

....

2 whole eggs
2 egg yolks
1 cup freshly grated Pecorino Romano cheese, plus more for sprinkling
¾ cup freshly grated Grana Padano or Parmigiano-Reggiano cheese
6 ounces pancetta or thick-cut bacon (not too smoky), cut into ¼-inch cubes or
    ¼-inch-wide strips
1 pound dried spaghetti, cooked al dente according to package directions
Salt and freshly ground black pepper

....

In a medium bowl, whisk together eggs and egg yolks. Whisk in cheese and ⅓ cup water. Set aside.

In a large skillet over medium heat, cook pancetta or bacon, stirring often, until lightly browned.

Remove skillet from heat and add pasta, tossing thoroughly to coat with fat.

Quickly add egg mixture and toss to coat the pasta with a creamy sauce; if necessary, add some warm water to thin the sauce. Season with salt and pepper and serve immediately, with grated cheese on the side.

Spaghetti and Meatballs

**SERVES 6–8 AS A FIRST COURSE OR SIDE DISH;
4–6 AS A MAIN COURSE**

There is no dish, perhaps, that better epitomizes Italian-American cuisine than spaghetti and meatballs. Meatballs actually originate in Italy, but it was Italian immigrants to America who dreamed up the combination with pasta. If you're not in the mood for spaghetti, these meatballs are just as delicious on hero rolls with tomato sauce and cheese.

....

To make the meatballs:

3 slices white bread, crusts removed

½ cup milk

1 pound ground chuck (not too lean)

2 cloves garlic, passed through a garlic press or smashed into a paste

¼ cup fresh Italian (flat leaf) parsley, finely chopped

1 cup freshly grated Parmigiano-Reggiano or Pecorino Romano

2 eggs, beaten

1 teaspoon salt

½ teaspoon pepper

1 tablespoon olive oil, plus more for greasing baking sheet

....

Preheat the oven to 400°F.

In a small mixing bowl, soak bread in milk for about 3 minutes. When it is soft, remove from the milk with your hands, squeeze out most of the milk, and tear into tiny pieces. In a large mixing bowl, use your hands to combine bread with the remaining ingredients, mixing thoroughly.

Wash hands and grease a baking sheet with oil. Dampen your hands with some warm water, and grab a small portion of meat from bowl. Roll between your palms to form a ball roughly 1¾ inches in diameter (about the size of a golf ball) and place ball on the baking sheet. Repeat until all meat is used up, and make sure the meatballs are not touching each other in the pan. Bake until they are light brown on the outside and almost cooked through on the inside, 15 to 18 minutes.

To assemble the dish:
Pomodoro sauce (see page 3)
1 pound dried spaghetti, cooked al dente according to package directions
Freshly grated Parmigiano-Reggiano or Pecorino Romano, for sprinkling

In a large saucepan over medium-high heat, bring sauce and meatballs to a simmer. Turn heat down to medium-low, cover the pot, and cook for 15 to 20 minutes.

Put spaghetti in a large serving bowl, and pour sauce and meatballs over the top. Serve with cheese on the side.

Tagliatelle alla Bolognese

**SERVES 6–8 AS A FIRST COURSE OR SIDE DISH;
4–6 AS A MAIN COURSE**

According to the late, great Italian cook Marcella Hazan, "There is no more perfect union in all gastronomy than the marriage of Bolognese ragù with homemade Bolognese tagliatelle." Bolognese sauce is all about the meat, which is just flavored with the vegetables and tomatoes. You can use packaged fresh tagliatelle to make your version of this splendid dish.

....

To make the ragù Bolognese:

3 tablespoons unsalted butter

½ medium onion, chopped

2 celery stalks, chopped

1 medium carrot, chopped

2 ounces pancetta or slab bacon, finely chopped

1 pound ground chuck (not too lean)

¼ teaspoon salt, plus more for adjusting seasoning

⅛ teaspoon freshly ground black pepper, plus more for adjusting seasoning

1 cup whole milk

⅛ teaspoon ground nutmeg

1 cup dry red wine

1 (14½-ounce) can pureed tomatoes

2 tablespoons tomato paste

....

In a large saucepan over medium heat, melt butter until it foams. Add onion and sauté until translucent, about 3 minutes. Add celery and carrot and sauté, stirring frequently, until crisp but somewhat tender, about 10 minutes. Add pancetta or bacon and beef, salt, and pepper. Cook, stirring and breaking the ground beef, until beef is no longer red, about 5 minutes.

Increase temperature to medium-high, add milk, nutmeg, and wine, and bring sauce to a rapid simmer. Cook, stirring often, until the fluid evaporates completely, about 5 minutes. Add tomatoes and tomato paste and stir until the sauce begins to bubble.

Reduce heat to low and simmer gently in the uncovered pot, stirring occasionally, for at least 3 hours. If the ragù starts to dry out, stir in ½ cup water when needed. The ragù should be thick and the meat should be very tender. Season with salt and pepper.

....

To assemble the dish:

1½ pounds fresh tagliatelle, cooked al dente according to package directions
2 tablespoons extra-virgin olive oil
Freshly grated Parmigiano-Reggiano or Pecorino Romano, for sprinkling

....

When the tagliatelle is ready, transfer it to a large serving bowl, drizzle on the oil, and spoon on the ragù. Toss and serve with cheese on the side.

Cheese Ravioli with Pesto

**SERVES 6 AS A FIRST COURSE OR SIDE DISH;
4 AS A MAIN COURSE**

This summery dish celebrates the flavors of central and southern Italy, where olives and herbs grow in profusion. Pesto brings those flavors together in a combination that pairs perfectly with ricotta. Use the freshest possible ravioli filled with fluffy ricotta—the frozen stuff tastes and feels leaden.

....

1½ pounds fresh cheese ravioli (plus ¼ cup cooking water)
1 cup pesto, prepared according to the Grilled Vegetable Panini recipe (see page 48)
Salt and freshly ground black pepper
Freshly grated Parmigiano-Reggiano or Pecorino Romano, for sprinkling

....

Cook ravioli according to package directions. When draining, reserve ¼ cup cooking water.

In a large serving bowl, spoon pesto over the ravioli and add 1 or 2 tablespoons of pasta water. Gently scoop the ravioli over onto itself to coat with the pesto. If the sauce isn't creamy enough, add a bit more water. Season with salt and pepper. Serve immediately with cheese on the side.

Meat Ravioli with Fontina Sauce and Walnuts

**SERVES 6 AS A FIRST COURSE OR SIDE DISH;
4 AS A MAIN COURSE**

If you're a meat-and-potatoes kind of person who's a little doubtful about pasta, give this robust, cheesy dish a whirl. It's guaranteed to stick to your ribs.

To make the fontina sauce:
6 tablespoons unsalted butter
½ cup heavy cream
½ pound fontina, grated
¼ cup freshly grated Parmigiano-Reggiano cheese
Salt and freshly ground black pepper

In a medium saucepan over medium heat, melt the butter. Stir in cream and bring almost to a boil. Slowly add the cheese, stirring constantly until it is melted and the sauce is smooth. Remove from heat immediately and season with salt and pepper.

To assemble the dish:
1½ pounds fresh meat ravioli, cooked according to package directions
½ cup toasted walnuts, roughly chopped

When the ravioli is ready, transfer it to a large serving bowl, and spoon the sauce over the top. Gently scoop the ravioli over onto itself to coat. Dish the ravioli into individual bowls and sprinkle walnuts on top. Serve immediately.

Squash or Pumpkin Ravioli with Brown Butter–Sage Sauce

**SERVES 6 AS A FIRST COURSE OR SIDE DISH;
4 AS A MAIN COURSE**

True to the traditions of northern Italy, this easy dish of fresh ravioli is dressed with butter rather than olive oil. Squash and pumpkin grow well in the north and can be used through the winter, unlike the seasonal tomatoes and vegetables of the south. The inclusion of fresh sage rather than dried is a must for this recipe.

....

To make the brown butter-sage sauce:
8 tablespoons (1 stick) unsalted butter, cut into tablespoon-size pieces
16 fresh sage leaves

....

Choose a medium stainless-steel saucepan without black or colored nonstick coating: You must be able to see the color of the butter sauce as it cooks. Put saucepan over medium-low heat and melt butter. Add sage and cook, stirring constantly, until butter turns golden and little brown bits appear on the bottom of the pan, about 3 minutes. Immediately remove from heat. The butter will continue cooking until it turns the toasty color of dark honey; any darker and it will taste bitter.

....

To assemble the dish:
1½ pounds fresh squash or pumpkin ravioli, cooked according to package directions
Salt and freshly ground black pepper

....

When the ravioli is ready, portion it into individual bowls. Spoon the sauce over the top, distributing the sage leaves equally. Serve with salt and pepper on the side.

Tortellini alla Panna with Pancetta and Peas

**SERVES 6 AS A FIRST COURSE OR SIDE DISH;
4 AS A MAIN COURSE**

The old Italian tale goes that tortellini's shape was inspired by Venus, the Roman goddess of love or maybe it was the famous Renaissance beauty Lucrezia Borgia. One them supposedly stopped for the night at a country inn. The innkeeper, smitten by his guest, peeked at her through the keyhole in her door. Alas, he could see no more than her navel, but he was so overcome by the sight that he ran to the kitchen and created a pasta in its shape: tortellini.

To make the panna sauce:

5 tablespoons unsalted butter

1½ cups heavy cream

¾ cup freshly grated Parmigiano-Reggiano, plus more for sprinkling

⅛ teaspoon ground nutmeg

Salt and freshly ground black pepper

In a large sauté pan over medium heat, melt 4 tablespoons butter into the cream. Bring mixture to a simmer and cook, stirring regularly, until it thickens slightly, about 1 minute.

Reduce heat to low and stir in the Parmigiano-Reggiano until it melts. Add the nutmeg and season with salt and pepper. Remove pot from the heat.

To assemble the dish:

1 cup fresh, shelled, or frozen peas

½ cup prosciutto, diced

1½ pounds fresh meat tortellini, cooked according to package directions

continued ▶

In a medium saucepan, steam peas for 2 minutes in a steaming basket over medium-high heat. Immediately remove peas from the pan and set aside.

Empty the pot of water, dry it, and return it to the stove over medium heat. Melt remaining 1 tablespoon butter. Add prosciutto and sauté until it sizzles but does not brown. Remove from heat and spoon the meat onto paper towels, leaving behind as much of the fat as possible. Stir the peas and prosciutto into the cream sauce.

Cook the tortellini according to package directions. When draining, reserve ¼ cup cooking water. Add tortellini to the cream sauce and stir gently to coat. Return the saucepan to the stove over low heat. Heat contents gently, stirring constantly, until hot (do not let it bubble), 2 to 4 minutes. If the sauce seems too thick, add 1 or 2 tablespoons pasta water. Serve immediately with pepper and cheese on the side.

Baked Ziti

SERVES 6–8 AS A MAIN COURSE

This Italian-American classic is a favorite of kids everywhere. This particular version uses ground beef, but you can substitute sausage or vegetables if you prefer.

....

To make the meat sauce:

2 tablespoons olive oil

2 garlic cloves, minced

1 pound ground chuck

1 batch pomodoro or marinara sauce (see page 2)

½ teaspoon fresh oregano, chopped

½ teaspoon fresh basil, chopped

⅛ teaspoon red pepper flakes

Salt and freshly ground black pepper

....

In a large saucepan over medium-high heat, heat oil and garlic, and sauté until garlic starts to sizzle, about 1 minute. Add the beef and cook until browned, breaking it up with the side of a spoon. Add the sauce, oregano, basil, and red pepper. Bring sauce to a simmer and cook uncovered for 30 minutes, stirring occasionally. Remove from heat and season with salt and pepper.

....

To assemble the dish:

1½ cups ricotta

2 cups (8 ounces) grated or shredded low-moisture mozzarella, divided

½ cup freshly grated Parmigiano-Reggiano

¾ pound ziti, cooked just short of al dente according to package directions

....

Preheat the oven to 350°F.

continued ▶

In a medium mixing bowl, combine ricotta, 1½ cups of the mozzarella, and Parmigiano-Reggiano. Add the ziti and toss to combine; then add 3 cups sauce and toss to combine.

Put the pasta in a 9-×-13-inch baking dish, spoon on remaining sauce, and sprinkle remaining cheese over top. Bake until it's bubbly, about 20 to 25 minutes.

Remove from oven and let ziti set for 5 to 10 minutes. Serve with cheese on the side.

Cannelloni with Béchamel Sauce

SERVES 4-6 AS A MAIN COURSE

You might be more familiar with the large filled pasta tubes called manicotti, but there's very little difference between that and cannelloni. Only the ultra-informed bother with the distinction, and indeed, you might only be able to find manicotti shells in your supermarket. No worries   you'll be pleased either way.

....

¼ cup (½ stick) unsalted butter, divided

1 pound fresh spinach, chopped

½ medium onion, finely chopped

1 pound ground veal

Salt

1 egg, beaten

¼ cup heavy cream

1 cup freshly grated Parmigiano-Reggiano, plus more for sprinkling

1 cup ricotta

¼ cup fresh Italian (flat leaf) parsley, chopped

⅛ teaspoon ground nutmeg

2 cups béchamel sauce, prepared according to the Broccoli and Cauliflower Gratin recipe (see page 67)

2 cups marinara sauce (see page 2)

12 dried cannelloni or manicotti tubes, cooked to just short of al dente according to package directions

....

In a large saucepan over medium heat, melt 2 tablespoons butter and add the spinach. Sauté until tender, about 5 minutes. Transfer to a bowl, leaving behind any liquid, and set aside. Discard the spinach liquid.

Return pan to the stove and melt remaining butter. Add onion and sauté until translucent, about 5 minutes. Add veal and about 1 teaspoon of salt and cook, breaking it up with the side of a spoon, until meat is no longer pink but not brown, about 5 minutes. Transfer meat to a large mixing bowl and allow to cool.

continued ▶

In a medium mixing bowl, blend together egg, cream, cheese, parsley, and nutmeg, and season with salt. Scoop the cheese mixture into the bowl with the cooled meat, and gently fold the ingredients together until just combined. Set the filling aside.

When the cannelloni tubes are cooked and drained, rinse under cold running water, pat dry, and lay out in a single layer on a dish towel so they are not touching. Cover with a damp—not wet—paper towel.

Preheat the oven to 400°F.

Spread ½ cup of the béchamel over the bottom of a 13-×-9-inch baking dish and dot with ½ cup of sauce. Lay a large sheet of waxed or parchment paper on a work surface.

Cut one corner off of a heavy-duty, quart-size plastic zipper bag, so there is an opening about ⅞-inch wide. Open the zipper end and, holding the small opening closed, scoop 2 to 3 cups of the filling into the bag. Seal the zipper end. Gently transfer 1 cannelloni tube from the towel to the work surface, and carefully insert a dinner knife, rotating it slowly to open the tube. Insert the open corner of the zipper bag into the tube and squeeze to fill. Leave about ¼ inch empty at each end. Lay the filled cannelloni in the baking dish, and repeat the process with the remaining tubes. The cannelloni should fit snugly next to one another in the dish.

Spoon remaining sauce over the cannelloni; then spoon the béchamel sauce over that. Use a spatula to smooth out the béchamel, and sprinkle the top with grated cheese. Bake until golden brown and bubbling, about 14 minutes. Let the cannelloni sit for 10 minutes before serving.

Lasagna

SERVES 6–8 AS A MAIN COURSE

Here's the recipe you've been waiting for. Whether you're feeding your family on a cold winter's night or taking a dish to a potluck, you can't go wrong with lasagna. There are two approaches to this favorite: The Italian-American, which piles on the cheese and sauce with no apologies, and the traditional Italian, made with béchamel sauce instead of mozzarella and ricotta for a lighter touch but just as much deliciousness. There's no denying it—this is the surefire American crowd-pleaser.

....

1 tablespoon olive oil

2 garlic cloves, chopped

1 pound sweet Italian sausage, slit open and filling removed

1 pound ground sirloin

Double recipe of pomodoro sauce (see page 3)

1 (15-ounce) container ricotta

2 eggs, beaten

½ cup fresh Italian (flat leaf) parsley, chopped

Salt and freshly grated black pepper

12 fresh or dried lasagna noodles, cooked to just short of al dente according to
   package directions

2¼ cups freshly grated Parmigiano-Reggiano

2¼ cups freshly grated low-moisture mozzarella

....

In a large saucepan over medium heat, heat olive oil and sauté garlic until it starts to sizzle; do not let it brown. Add sausage filling and beef and brown well. Drain excess fat from the pot, but do not scrape the bottom. Stir in the sauce and bring to a simmer. Cover and cook for 30 minutes, stirring occasionally. Remove from heat.

In a medium mixing bowl, combine ricotta, egg, and parsley. Season with salt and pepper.

When the lasagna noodles are cooked and drained, rinse under cold running water, pat dry, and lay in a single layer on a dish towel so they are not touching. Cover with a damp—not wet—paper towel.

continued ▶

Build the lasagna: Spread 1½ cups meat sauce on the bottom of a 9-×-13-inch baking dish. Lay 4 noodles on top of the sauce. Dot the noodles with half of the ricotta mixture; then sprinkle on ¾ cup Parmigiano-Reggiano and ¾ cup mozzarella. Repeat process for the second layer. For the top layer, lay 4 noodles over the second layer, and spoon on 1½ cups meat sauce. Scatter the remaining ¾ cup Parmigiano-Reggiano and ¾ cup mozzarella on top.

Tent a sheet of foil over the top of the baking dish so it doesn't touch the cheese. Place dish on a baking sheet, and bake lasagna for 40 minutes. Remove foil and continue baking for 15 to 20 minutes, allowing the top to brown lightly. Remove lasagna from the oven and let it sit for 15 minutes before cutting and serving.

Stuffed Shells

SERVES 4–6 AS A MAIN COURSE

Lasagna a little too much work for you? Stuffed shells are equally yummy, but quicker to make and lighter in the tummy. They're also a great vegetarian option.

....

2 pounds ricotta cheese

3 eggs, beaten

1½ cups freshly grated low-moisture mozzarella, divided

1½ cups freshly grated Parmigiano-Reggiano, divided plus more for sprinkling

¼ cup fresh Italian (flat-leaf) parsley, chopped

Salt and freshly grated black pepper

One 12-ounce package dried jumbo pasta shells, cooked to just short of al dente according to package directions

2½ cups marinara sauce (see page 2)

....

Preheat the oven to 375°F.

In a large mixing bowl, thoroughly combine ricotta, eggs, ¾ cup mozzarella, ¾ cup Parmigiano-Reggiano, and parsley. Season with salt and pepper.

When the shells are cooked and drained, rinse under cold running water, pat dry, and lay in a single layer on a dish towel, open side down. Cover with a damp—not wet—paper towel.

Spread 1 cup sauce over the bottom of a 9-×-13-inch baking dish. Holding a shell in the palm of one hand, scoop some of the cheese mixture into the shell to fill completely. Place the stuffed shell in the baking dish, open side up. Repeat with all shells. The shells should fit snugly together in the dish. Spoon the remaining sauce over top of the shells. Scatter remaining Parmigiano-Reggiano across the top, then remaining mozzarella.

Tent a sheet of foil over the top of the baking dish so it doesn't touch the cheese. Place dish on a baking sheet and bake shells for 40 minutes. Remove foil and continue baking for 10 to 15 minutes, until cheese is bubbling. Remove dish from the oven and let the shells sit for 5 to 10 minutes before serving.

Basic Risotto

SERVES 6 AS A FIRST COURSE OR SIDE DISH

Risotto is kind of like an upscale version of rice pilaf, that predictable side dish served next to vegetable medleys in chain restaurants. It's cooked in a broth for flavor and may include a variety of ingredients such as wine, herbs, vegetables, or seafood. But risotto ain't no Rice-A-Roni! It's a masterpiece of northern Italian cookery, a sophisticated dish of subtle flavors, well-integrated ingredients, and uniquely creamy texture that comes from the very special rice from which it's made. Risotto, such as this classic rendition, is typically served as a primi, *but its more substantial versions are often served as a main course.*

....

1 quart low-sodium beef, chicken, or vegetable broth (homemade is far superior)
5 tablespoons unsalted butter
1 small onion, very finely chopped
2 cups arborio rice
¾ cup freshly grated Parmigiano-Reggiano
Salt

....

In a medium saucepan over medium-high heat, bring the broth plus 1 cup water to a simmer. Reduce heat to medium-low and keep the broth simmering while you cook the risotto. In a large saucepan over medium-high heat, melt butter until it foams and add onion. Sauté onion until it is translucent but does not brown, about 2 minutes. Add the rice and stir to toast it and coat it with the butter, 3 to 4 minutes.

Keep heat at medium and ladle ½ cup hot broth into the pot with the rice. With a long wooden spoon, stir without stopping, frequently scraping down the sides of the pot and scraping off the bottom to keep the rice from sticking. When the rice has absorbed the broth, after about 3 minutes, add another ½ cup liquid and repeat process. Continue the routine, stirring constantly, for another 15 minutes, then start checking the texture of the rice. If it is not yet al dente, keep adding liquid and stirring as you have been. Check the texture every few minutes. If you run out of broth before the rice is al dente, continue cooking with hot water as the liquid. As soon as the rice is al dente, remove pot from the heat. Season with salt if needed and serve in bowls.

VARIATION: SIMPLE ADDITIONS

....

¾ cup freshly grated Parmigiano-Reggiano

....

Stir the cheese into the risotto when the rice is 2 minutes short of al dente.

....

1 ounce dried porcini mushrooms

....

Soak the mushrooms in 2 cups of warm water for 30 minutes. Add mushrooms and ½ cup of their liquid to the risotto once it has been cooking for 10 minutes. Use ½-cup portions of the liquid in place of the ladles of broth for the next few rounds of the cooking process, until you have used all of it up; then continue with the broth per the original recipe.

....

1 pound asparagus

....

Before starting the risotto, boil the asparagus in 1 quart water for 5 minutes. Remove asparagus from the pot and add 2 cups broth to the water. Heat the liquid to a simmer. Cut asparagus into ½-inch pieces and add to the pot when you put in the onion. Use asparagus-broth mixture to make the risotto.

....

1½ cups Ragù Bolognese (prepared according to the Tagliatelle alla Bolognese Recipe earlier)

....

Leave out the onion in the Basic Risotto recipe, and put the sauce in the pot before the rice. Stir rice into the sauce, and make the risotto using beef broth. Add ⅓ cup grated Parmigiano-Reggiano at the end, if desired.

Risotto alla Milanese

SERVES 6 AS A FIRST COURSE OR SIDE DISH

This is the risotto to end all risottos—the classic dish of Milan, the northern Italian city that reputedly invented risotto. There's even a legend about Risotto alla Milanese: The story goes that in 1574, when the city's duomo *(cathedral) was under construction, a glassmaker's apprentice was in the habit of brightening the colors of stained glass by adding saffron to the dyes. His master joked that the young man would put saffron in anything—including his food. In return, the apprentice snuck some saffron into the rice that was to be served at the master's wedding. It turned out that the yellow rice was delicious!*

....

1 teaspoon saffron strands
1 quart low-sodium chicken broth
¼ cup extra-virgin olive oil
1 small onion, finely minced
2 ounces pancetta or bacon, diced
2 cups arborio rice
1½ cups dry white wine
3 tablespoons unsalted butter
½ cup freshly grated Parmigiano-Reggiano
Salt

....

Dissolve the saffron in 1 cup hot water. In a medium saucepan over medium-high heat, bring broth to a simmer and add saffron water. Reduce heat to medium-low and keep liquid simmering while you cook the risotto.

In a large saucepan over medium-high heat, heat oil and add onion and pancetta. Sauté until onion is translucent but does not brown, about 2 minutes. Add rice and stir to toast it and coat it with the oil, 3 to 4 minutes. Keep heat at medium-high and pour in the wine. Stir constantly with a long wooden spoon until rice absorbs the wine.

Ladle ½ cup hot broth into the pan with the rice. Stir without stopping, frequently scraping down the sides of the pan and scraping off the bottom to keep the rice from sticking. When the rice has absorbed the broth, about 3 minutes, add another

½ cup liquid and repeat the process. Continue the routine, stirring constantly, for another 15 minutes; then start checking the texture of the rice. If it is not yet al dente, keep adding liquid and stirring as you have been. Check the texture every few minutes. If you run out of broth before rice is al dente, continue cooking with water as hot as the liquid.

As soon as the rice is al dente, add butter and cheese and stir vigorously until both have melted. Remove pot from the heat and season with salt if needed. Serve in bowls.

Seafood Risotto

It's no surprise that Venice, situated in a lagoon of the Adriatic Sea, would claim seafood risotto as one of its culinary specialties. Risotto with eels is a Christmas tradition, but this recipe sticks with shrimp. Phew!

2 cups clam juice

7 tablespoons butter, divided

2 large shallots, finely chopped

2 garlic cloves, minced

2 cups arborio rice

1½ cups dry white wine

½ cup fresh lemon juice

1½ pounds uncooked tiny or extra-small shrimp, fresh or thawed

¼ cup parsley, finely chopped

Zest of 1 large lemon

Salt and freshly ground black pepper

In a medium saucepan over medium-high heat, combine clam juice with 3 cups water and bring to a simmer. Reduce heat to medium-low and keep the liquid simmering while you cook the risotto.

In a large saucepan over medium-high heat, melt 5 tablespoons butter and add shallots and garlic. Sauté until shallots are translucent but do not brown, about 2 minutes. Add the rice and stir to toast it and coat it with the oil, 3 to 4 minutes. Keep the heat at medium-high and pour in the wine. Stir constantly with a long wooden spoon until rice absorbs the wine.

Ladle ½ cup hot broth into the pan with the rice. Stir without stopping, frequently scraping down the sides of the pan and scraping off the bottom to keep the rice from sticking. When the rice has absorbed the broth, about 3 minutes, add another ½ cup liquid and repeat the process. Continue the routine, stirring constantly, for another 10 minutes; then stir in the lemon juice with the next ½ cup liquid. Cook for 5 minutes; then start checking the texture of the rice. If it is not yet al dente, keep adding liquid and stirring as you have been. Check the texture every few minutes. If you run out of broth before rice is al dente, continue cooking with water as the liquid.

As the rice approaches al dente, stir in the shrimp, parsley, and lemon zest. Again, continue the risotto process, and when the rice is fully al dente, add remaining 2 tablespoons butter and stir to melt. Remove pot from the heat and season with salt and pepper. Serve in bowls.

CHAPTER 7

Fish and Shellfish

Pesce (fish) and *frutti di mare* (shellfish, literally "fruits of the sea") are beloved fare in Italy. After all, the country has 5,000 miles of coastline bordering the Mediterranean and Adriatic seas, whose warm, salty waters teem with underwater creatures. Italy's many lakes, rivers, and streams abound with fish and shellfish, too. Italians have been taking advantage of these phenomenal resources and dining on aquatic delicacies since time immemorial, so they've had plenty of time to perfect countless ways to cook everything that comes out of the water. Today, the diverse seafood dishes of Italy are celebrated worldwide.

And what variety! Tuna (*tonno*), swordfish (*pesce spada*), and salmon (*salmone*); branzino, sea bream (*orata*), and tilapia; anchovies (*alice*), sardines (*sardine*), and mullet (*cefalo*); squid (*calamari*), octopus (*polpo*), and cuttlefish (*seppie*); clams (*vongole*), mussels (*cozze, mitili*), and oysters (*ostrice*); shrimp (*gamberi, gamber-etti*), prawns (*gambarelli*), and lobster (*aragosta*): These are only a very few of the sea creatures you'll find in Italian cookery.

There's just as much range in the techniques used to prepare these tasty beasts. In the kitchen, they're broiled, fried, baked, grilled, boiled, steamed, and poached. They're included in antipasti, soups, stews, salads, and sandwiches; served as *primi* (in pasta and risotto dishes) and *secondi* (on their own); and sold fresh, frozen, tinned, dried, and salted. There's even a fish egg product called *bottarga*: The eggs (from tuna or mullet) are dried and cured in salt to yield a hard block, which is shaved over certain dishes to punch up the flavor.

Italian-American cuisine makes just as much use of seafood, especially around Roman Catholic holidays such as Lent (and every Monday and Friday) that require abstinence from pleasures such as meat. There's no pleasure lost, though, in the wonderful seafood creations that reflect this tradition, most spectacularly in the Feast of the Seven Fishes. On Christmas Eve, families share a meal that consists of seven different seafood dishes—though some interpret the feast differently, featuring ten or even thirteen offerings. Usually, the menu assembles very traditional dishes, though there seem to be as many interpretations of the feast as there are families who celebrate it. Most seem to agree that *baccalà* (dried salt cod) and eel should be part of the picture, but then the menu may branch out to *fritto misto* (mixed fried seafood), calamari salad, clams casino, shrimp scampi, a spicy shellfish *fra diavolo,* a pasta dish, a fish stew, a sautéed fillet, or whole roasted fish.

All this fishy abundance means that you've got limitless possibilities for creating stunning Italian-style fish and shellfish dishes. Have fun with them!

How to Buy Fish

At the fish counter in your supermarket you'll find fish in many forms: fillets, steaks, and whole; fresh and previously frozen/thawed; and some live critters. The first and most important rule to follow when choosing what's for dinner is to ask the fishmonger what's freshest, preferably what came in that day. If there's no one to ask, or if you can't get a straight answer, look for a few things:

- Prepackaged seafood should be labeled with packed-on and sell-by dates. Choose the package with the latest dates, and reject anything that's expired. If you can, go for the unwrapped stuff on ice behind the counter.

- Cuts and whole fish should glisten with moisture and must not show any dryness.

- Anything you're considering must smell fresh, like the sea, and not fishy (go ahead—ask to smell it!).

- Whole fish must have clear eyes and red gills (again, ask to take a look); fish that hasn't been cleaned and gutted stays fresher longer than fish that has been processed before you select it.

- In general, whole fish (and fish cut in large chunks) stays fresher longer than precut fillets. You can ask your fishmonger to fillet or cut these into steaks for you.

- Shrimp should be raw and unshelled.

- Lobster must be alive, in a clean, well-aerated tank of water: Make sure it squirms energetically when picked up.

- The shells of clams, mussels, and oysters must be tightly shut and undamaged: If the shell is open, the mollusk is dead and absolutely must not be eaten.

- Frozen seafood should not show any signs of freezer burn.

Cooking Seafood

Even the best ingredients can ruin a recipe if they're not cooked and served properly. There are four simple things you can do to help make your seafood dishes the very best they can be:

1. Before using it, rinse your seafood thoroughly under cold running water, and pat it dry with paper towels. This will remove any stray scales and make the flavor super-fresh.

2. Gently feel through fillets for fine bones. If you find any, pull them out with your fingers or clean needle-nose pliers. You don't want anyone choking at the table!

3. Don't cook fish, shrimp, or lobster all the way through (mollusks are a whole other story). The seafood will continue cooking after you remove it from the heat, and the last thing you want is dried-out, chewy meat.

4. Don't melt or sprinkle cheese on seafood. These two flavors don't enhance each other at all, and combining them is an absolute no-no in Italian cooking.

Whole Branzino, Roasted or Grilled

SERVES 2

*The branzino — aka branzini, bronzini, loup de mer, and European sea bass — lives
wild in the Mediterranean Sea and is also farmed in the waters surrounding Italy.
With silver sides and a white belly, it's a relatively small fish, perfect for two servings.
The flesh is white and firm, with a mild flavor, and it has few of those pesky pin bones
to worry about.*

....

1 pound whole branzino, cleaned, gutted, and scaled, head left on
Extra-virgin olive oil
Sea salt and freshly ground black pepper
5 fresh thyme sprigs
5 fresh sage sprigs
1 large lemon, half cut into thin slices and half into 4 wedges
10 whole kalamata olives, pitted and halved
10 cherry tomatoes, halved

....

Preheat the oven to 400°F or the grill to medium.

Rinse fish inside and out and pat dry. Score the skin on both sides with ¼-inch-
deep cuts spaced about 1½ inches apart. Rub outside of the fish with olive oil.
Sprinkle outside and inside with salt and pepper.

Stuff with the thyme and sage. If grilling, stuff lemon slices into the fish as well.

If roasting: Oil a 9-×-13-inch baking pan and lay lemon slices in a row. Place fish
in the pan on top of lemon slices. Cook until fish is just opaque in the center, 20 to
25 minutes.

If grilling: Oil grill rack and place fish in the center. Cook on first side until skin no
longer sticks to the rack, 5 to 7 minutes. Flip fish over and cook until just opaque in
the center, 5 to 7 minutes.

Remove herbs from the fish and discard. Remove lemon slices from pan or inside of
the fish and lay half on each of two dinner plates.

continued ▶

Peel skin off the top side of the fish and discard. Insert a knife between the flesh and the bones and run it along the length of the fish to remove flesh. Pick any remaining flesh from the bones. Cut the cheek out of the head. Place all flesh on top of the lemons on one of the dinner plates. Flip the fish and repeat procedure on the other side, placing the meat on the second dinner plate.

Scatter half the olives and tomatoes onto the fish on each plate. Place half lemon wedges next to the fish on each plate for squeezing. Serve with salt and pepper on the side.

Salmon with Lemon, Capers, and Rosemary

SERVES 4

Salmon isn't native to the Mediterranean, and Italians started eating it only recently. But even though they must import all of their salmon, it has become a well-established part of the cuisine.

....

4 (6-ounce) salmon fillets, cut from the thick part of the slab

Sea salt and freshly ground black pepper

3 tablespoons unsalted butter, divided

2 tablespoons extra-virgin olive oil

1 cup dry white wine

Juice of 1 large lemon

¼ cup capers, drained

Zest of 1 large lemon

....

Rinse the fillets and pat them dry; then lightly sprinkle both sides with salt and pepper.

In a large skillet over medium-high heat, melt 1 tablespoon butter into the olive oil and heat until hot but not smoking. Place fillets in pan skin-side down, and sear until skin is crispy, 2 to 3 minutes. Reduce heat to medium and gently turn over fillets to brown other side. Cook to medium-rare: The flesh in the center should still be translucent, but will continue cooking after you remove from heat. Using a spatula, carefully transfer the fish to a warm plate and cover with foil or a pot lid.

Pour the wine and lemon juice into pan and deglaze, cooking while scraping the brown bits off bottom of pan into the liquid. Cook until liquid reduces by half. Swirl in the remaining 2 tablespoons butter and add capers and lemon zest.

Carefully place each salmon fillet on a separate dinner plate, making sure not to break up the fish. Pour sauce over the top and serve with salt and pepper on the side.

Red Snapper Livornese

SERVES 4

This boldly flavored dish comes from the city of Livorno, on the coast of southern Tuscany. If you don't have time to make the marinara, substitute whole canned plum tomatoes and throw in a clove or two of chopped garlic.

2 tablespoons extra-virgin olive oil

1 small yellow onion, diced

2 cups marinara sauce (see page 2)

1 cup dry white wine

¾ cup Gaeta olives

¼ cup capers, drained

1 teaspoon red pepper flakes, dried (optional)

Sea salt and freshly ground black pepper

4 (6-ounce) red snapper fillets

Preheat the oven to 400°F.

In a large ovenproof skillet over medium heat, heat olive oil and add onion. Cook until onion is translucent, about 5 minutes. Add marinara sauce, wine, olives, capers, and red pepper (if using) and bring to a boil.

While sauce is heating, rinse fillets and pat them dry. Season the sauce with salt and black pepper. Place fillets in the skillet skin side up and spoon some sauce over the top. Slide skillet into the oven and bake until the fish is just cooked through, 10 to 15 minutes.

Using a spatula, gently transfer each fillet to a separate dinner plate. Spoon sauce over the top, and serve with salt and pepper on the side.

Sicilian Swordfish

SERVES 4

Sicily is famous for its swordfish, whose meaty texture is an ideal vehicle for the intense flavors of the local produce. Not surprisingly, there are many, many recipes you could call Sicilian Swordfish. This one takes a solid, basic approach.

2 tablespoons golden raisins
¼ cup extra-virgin olive oil, divided
1 medium onion, halved and sliced into thin crescents
1 garlic clove, chopped
1 celery rib, sliced into thin crescents
¼ cup oil-cured black olives, pitted and coarsely chopped
2 tablespoons capers, drained and coarsely chopped
⅛ teaspoon dried red pepper flakes
½ cup dry white wine
1 pound tomatoes, cored, seeded, and coarsely chopped, with juice
Sea salt and freshly ground black pepper
4 (6-ounce) swordfish steaks, about ¾ inch thick

In a small bowl, cover raisins with hot water and soak for 1 minute; then drain, reserving the water.

In a large skillet heat 2 tablespoons oil over medium-high heat and add onion, garlic, and celery. Cook, stirring often, until onion is lightly brown and celery has softened, 3 to 4 minutes. Add raisins, olives, capers, and red pepper and cook for 2 minutes. Pour in the raisin water and wine, and add the tomatoes with their juices. Cover the skillet, reduce heat to medium-low, and simmer for 10 minutes. Uncover the pan and simmer for 10 additional minutes to reduce sauce. Season sauce with salt and pepper and transfer to a medium mixing bowl. Set aside.

Rinse fish, pat dry, and lightly season with salt and pepper. Increase heat under skillet to medium-high and add oil. When oil is hot but not smoking, lay steaks in the pan. Cook until lightly browned and medium-rare, about 3 minutes per side.

continued ▶

When the fish is ready, reduce heat to medium and pour sauce back into the pan. Heat until sauce just starts to bubble. With a spatula, gently remove each steak to its own dinner plate. Spoon sauce over the fish and serve with salt and pepper on the side.

Tuna alla Genovese

SERVES 6

The northern Italian city of Genoa lies on a bay of the Mediterranean that's known as the Ligurian Sea. Over the centuries the Genoese have become renowned for their seafood dishes, such as this classic.

....

1 ounce porcini mushrooms, dried
6 tablespoons extra-virgin olive oil, divided
3 garlic cloves, finely chopped
1 medium onion, finely chopped
2 anchovy fillets, finely chopped
2 tablespoons freshly squeezed lemon juice
1½ cups dry white wine
1 teaspoon fresh thyme, chopped
Sea salt and freshly ground black pepper
2 tablespoons fresh parsley, chopped
6 (6-ounce) tuna steaks, at least 1 inch thick
½ cup all-purpose flour

....

In a small bowl, soak porcini in 2 cups warm water for about 30 minutes. Remove pieces from water, reserving liquid. Finely chop mushrooms.

In a large skillet over medium-high heat, heat 2 tablespoons oil and add porcini, garlic, onion, and anchovy. Sauté, mashing anchovy into a paste with the back of a spoon, until garlic is sizzling and onion is lightly browned. Pour in lemon juice, wine, and porcini water; then add thyme and season with salt and pepper. Bring sauce to a boil and cook, stirring often, until it reduces by half. Reduce heat to low, stir in parsley, and cover pan.

Rinse fish and pat it dry. Lightly sprinkle the fish with salt and pepper on all sides. In a large skillet over medium-high heat, heat 4 tablespoons oil. Spread flour on a plate and dredge tuna steaks to coat lightly, shaking off excess flour.

continued ▶

When oil is hot, place fish in the pan. Cook fish until it is lightly browned, about 1 minute on each side; it should still be rare on the inside. Put the browned steaks into the pan that contains the sauce. Heat on each side for 1 to 2 minutes for rare, longer if you want the fish less rare. With a spatula, gently remove each steak to its own dinner plate and spoon sauce over the top. Serve with salt and pepper on the side.

Stuffed Calamari

SERVES 4

You can stuff calamari with just about anything, from crab to sausage to chopped veggies. Many recipes call for frying the squid in oil, but this lighter approach bakes them in the oven. Just don't overstuff the tubes: The squid will shrink while cooking and the stuffing needs space to expand.

12 large, cleaned squid

4 cups bread crumbs

1 cup freshly grated Parmigiano-Reggiano or Pecorino Romano, plus more for sprinkling

4 garlic cloves, minced

½ cup Italian (flat leaf) parsley, chopped, plus more for garnish

¼ cup olive oil, plus more for greasing pan

2 eggs, beaten

Sea salt and freshly ground black pepper

2 cups marinara sauce (see page 2)

Preheat the oven to 350°F.

Rinse calamari tubes inside and out and pat dry. If you also have tentacles, chop them up. In a medium mixing bowl, combine bread crumbs, cheese, garlic, parsley, and tentacles (if using). Mix in oil and eggs, and season with salt and pepper.

Grease a 9-×-13-inch baking dish with oil. Use a spoon to fill a squid tube with stuffing, pushing it in so it is cohesive but not packed. Leave about ½ inch unfilled at the open end. Close the tube with a toothpick and lay it in the baking dish. Repeat for all 12 tubes.

Bake squid for 10 minutes; then remove from oven and spoon marinara sauce over the top. Return dish to the oven and bake for another 12 minutes. Remove from oven, sprinkle with cheese, and garnish with parsley. Allow the calamari to sit for about 5 minutes; then remove toothpicks and serve.

Baked Clams Oreganata

SERVES 4

You can serve these clams as an appetizer (to serve 6 to 8), but they're such yummy comfort food you just may want them as a secondo after a pasta course.

....

20 live littleneck clams

¾ cup plain bread crumbs

3 tablespoons freshly grated Parmigiano-Reggiano

2 cloves garlic, finely chopped

1 tablespoon fresh oregano, chopped, or 2 teaspoons dried

2 tablespoons fresh parsley, chopped, or 2 teaspoons dried

¼ cup extra-virgin olive oil, plus more for finishing

Salt and freshly ground black pepper

1 lemon, cut into 8 wedges

....

Move broiler pan to middle rung under the broiler. Preheat the oven to 450°F.

Do not purchase clams with damaged shells or shells that are not tightly shut. Before cooking, re-check clams and discard any that have opened. You should end up with at least 16 live clams. Scrub clams under cold running water to remove any barnacles, seaweed, and sand, and place on a baking sheet in a single layer. Bake in the oven (not the broiler) until they just start to open, 2 to 3 minutes. Remove from oven and let cool until they can be handled. Discard any clams that have not opened.

Turn the oven to broil. Working over a small bowl to catch the clam juice, hold a clam in the palm of one hand, and use a butter knife to pry it open. Discard top shell and carefully detach meat from the bottom shell. Strain clam juice through cheesecloth or a very fine sieve to get rid of any sand or other debris.

In a medium mixing bowl toss bread crumbs, cheese, garlic, oregano, and parsley until just combined. Stir in oil and 2 tablespoons clam juice. Season with salt and pepper.

Use a tablespoon to top clams with the crumb mixture. Pat crumbs down gently so they stay in place—but don't pack them—and drizzle with oil. Place clams on the broiler pan and broil until topping is crisp and golden brown, 4 to 5 minutes. Serve with lemon wedges on the side.

Mussels Fra Diavolo

SERVES 4

Fra Diavolo (Italian for "brother devil") was an eighteenth-century guerilla who fought the French occupiers of the southern Italian city of Naples. Originated by Italian immigrants to the United States, the sauce that bears his name is as hot and fiery as he was.

5 pounds live mussels

1 batch pomodoro sauce (see page 3)

1½ teaspoons red pepper flakes, crushed

3 red chiles, dried

1 (8-ounce) bottle clam juice

1½ cups dry white wine, divided

Salt and freshly ground black pepper

1 tablespoon olive oil

3 shallots, finely chopped

Do not purchase mussels with damaged shells. The freshest mussels tend to be tightly closed, but open shells do not necessarily mean mussels are dead. Store live mussels in a large, dry mixing bowl in the refrigerator, covered with a damp towel so they can breathe, until you are ready to use them.

In a large saucepan over medium-high heat, combine pomodoro sauce, red pepper flakes, dried chiles, clam juice, and ½ cup wine. Season with salt and black pepper. Bring sauce to a boil, partially cover the pot, and lower heat to medium-low. Simmer sauce for 30 to 45 minutes, stirring occasionally.

While sauce is cooking, recheck mussels to make sure they are alive: Pick them up, squeeze gently, and tap on a work surface. Discard any that do not close when squeezed or tapped. Hold each live mussel in your hand, and with a dish towel or paper towel, sharply tug the clump of hairs—the beard—down toward the hinge of the shell to pull it off. Scrub mussels under cold running water to remove any barnacles, seaweed, and sand. Put each mussel in a mixing bowl filled with cold water—if it floats, discard it. Immediately remove live mussels from water; you

continued ▶

should end up with at least 4 pounds. Store mussels in the refrigerator, covered with a damp towel, until you are ready to cook them.

In a wide saucepan with high sides, heat oil over medium heat and add shallots. Cook for 1 minute, stirring constantly. Stir in remaining cup of wine and spicy pomodoro sauce. Bring sauce to a boil and add mussels. Stir to coat, cover pot, and cook until shells open, 3 to 5 minutes. Discard any mussels that have not opened.

Transfer mussels to 4 large individual bowls and spoon sauce over the top. Serve with an additional large bowl for discarding empty shells while eating.

Shrimp Scampi

SERVES 4

The name of this dish is a little confusing. Sometimes "scampi" is used as the general name for shrimp in any dish. Sometimes it's used as the name of this preparation, which can also be made with prawns or lobster. But whatever you call it, you'll call it delicious. It's easiest to buy shrimp that are already cleaned, either fresh or frozen (but not precooked).

....

2 pounds extra jumbo (16–20 count) shrimp (total 32–40 shrimp), shelled and deveined

2 sticks (1 cup) unsalted butter

6 garlic cloves, minced

1 cup dry white wine

¼ cup freshly squeezed lemon juice

2 tablespoons fresh parsley, chopped

Salt and freshly ground black pepper

....

Rinse shrimp and pat dry.

In a large skillet over medium heat, melt butter and cook garlic until soft but not browned, 1 to 2 minutes. Add the wine and lemon juice and simmer until sauce reduces slightly, 3 to 4 minutes.

Add shrimp and parsley and cook for 2 minutes; then turn them over and continue cooking until they turn pink, 1 to 2 minutes. Do not allow the shrimp to get very firm or they will be tough and rubbery. Remove pan from heat and season with salt and pepper. Serve alone or over pasta.

Cioppino

SERVES 4-6

If you've ever been to Fisherman's Wharf in San Francisco, you'll have come across cioppino. That's where Italian-American fishermen invented it in the nineteenth century, and that's where it's still the signature dish, sometimes served in sourdough bread bowls. It's a fish stew that can contain anything from crab and shrimp to clams and mussels to fish and squid. This recipe has a lot of ingredients, but if you buy all of your seafood pre-cleaned it's easy to make—and easy to eat!

....

6 tablespoons olive oil, divided

1 large onion, halved and sliced into thin crescents

2 celery stalks, cut into thin crescents

5 cloves garlic, halved

3 dried bay leaves

½ cup chopped fresh parsley

1 tablespoon fresh oregano, chopped, or 1 teaspoon, dried

½ teaspoon red pepper flakes

2 (28-ounce) cans tomatoes, crushed

1 (8-ounce) bottle clam juice

Sea salt and freshly ground black pepper

1 tablespoon unsalted butter

1 clove garlic, minced

1 cup dry white wine

1 pound mild, firm-fleshed fish, such as cod, haddock, halibut, or pollock, cut into
    1- to 2-inch cubes

½ pound squid, tentacles separated and tubes cut into ½-inch rings

½ pound bay (small) scallops

½ pound medium shrimp, shelled and deveined

2 (6-ounce) cans lump or claw crab meat

....

In a large saucepan over medium heat, heat 4 tablespoons olive oil. Add onions and sauté until translucent. Add celery, halved garlic cloves, bay leaves, parsley, oregano, and red pepper flakes and cook, stirring, until celery is soft, about 5 minutes. Stir in tomatoes and clam juice. Bring to boil, reduce heat to low-medium, and simmer uncovered for about 1 hour. Season with salt and black pepper.

In a large saucepan over medium heat, melt butter into the remaining 2 table-spoons oil and add minced garlic. Cook, stirring, until garlic is fragrant but not browned. Add wine and prepared tomato-clam sauce. Bring to a boil, reduce heat to medium-low, cover, and simmer, stirring occasionally, for 20 minutes.

Increase heat to medium, add fish, squid, and scallops; bring pot to a simmer; and cook, stirring frequently, until fish just cooks through. Add shrimp, return pot to a simmer, cover, and cook for 5 more minutes. Stir in crab and cook until it is just warmed through, 1 to 2 minutes. Serve in bowls with crusty sourdough bread on the side.

CHAPTER 8

Poultry and Meats

If you're interested in Italian food, you've no doubt heard about the "Mediterranean Diet," that ideal nutritional regimen that's thought to reduce your risk of heart disease and cancer and increase your chances of living a long, long time, all while keeping your waistline trim. The menu includes lots of vegetables and fruit, beans, unrefined grains, fish, and olive oil, and not so much dairy, or meat, including poultry. Up to a point, Italians do eat this way, although they also love their pasta and bread, and in the north they throw in plenty of butter instead of olive oil. For the most part, though, the traditional Italian diet is exceptionally healthy. But that's not why Italians eat the way they do: They simply eat what's freshest, tastiest, handiest, and cheapest, and that just happens to be the stuff that's good for you.

The upshot is that the typical Italian fills up on veggies, with animal protein as a nice extra. And when it comes to protein, Italy has always relied heavily on seafood from the seas that surround its boot and islands. Poultry, pork, and beef play much smaller roles than they do on the American plate. Worldwide, Italy ranks twenty-third in per-capita consumption of poultry, fifteenth in consumption of pork, and ninth in consumption of beef. Compare that to America, where the typical person eats more meat than anyone else on earth, except for the citizens of Luxembourg!

Even though they eat less of it, however, Italians really do enjoy meat, and they've created many wonderful ways of preparing it. In the *secondo*—the meat course—quality is more important than quantity, so portions are smaller than in the United States and recipes focus on maximizing the flavors of meat and poultry in harmony with vegetables, herbs, olive oil, and seasonings. For the most part, the dishes in the *secondo* are refined and sophisticated rather than big and hearty.

That doesn't mean that hardcore carnivores are out of luck, especially since Italian-Americans have adapted the recipes of the Old World to the appetites of the New. This chapter offers you a few from each side of the pond.

Chicken Cacciatore

SERVES 4–6

Cacciatore is the Italian word for "hunter," and it's said that this dish originated with hunters who prepared their game in the field with whatever other ingredients were at hand. They'd throw poultry or rabbit in a pot with onions, tomatoes, and herbs, and maybe some carrots, bell peppers, or mushrooms; then pour in some wine and set the pot in the fire to braise low and slow. The result is fall-off-the-bone tender. This is a stove-top recipe, but you can prepare it in a slow cooker, too.

....

1 (3 to 4-pound) chicken cut up into parts, or an equal weight of precut, bone-in parts
¾ cup all-purpose flour
1 teaspoon salt, plus more for seasoning
½ teaspoon freshly ground black pepper, plus more for seasoning
¼ cup olive oil
1 large onion, halved and sliced into very thin crescents
¾ cup dry white wine
2 garlic cloves, minced
1 teaspoon fresh sage, chopped
1 teaspoon fresh thyme, chopped
1 medium carrot, diced
2 celery stalks, sliced into thin crescents
1 red, yellow, or orange bell pepper, seeded, de-ribbed, and diced
½ cup white or cremini mushrooms, sliced
1 (28-ounce) can tomatoes, with juice, diced

....

Rinse the chicken parts and pat them dry. Combine flour, salt, and black pepper on a plate and spread out. Dredge chicken parts in the flour to coat thoroughly but lightly, shaking off excess.

In a large saucepan over medium-high heat, heat oil until hot but not smoking. Place chicken in the pot, skin side down, and brown it; then flip over and brown the other side. You may have to do this in batches. Set the browned chicken aside.

continued ▶

Reduce heat to medium and add onion to the pot. Sauté until onion is golden, about 10 minutes. Pour in wine and deglaze the pot, scraping any brown bits from the bottom and sides into the liquid. Add garlic, sage, thyme, carrot, celery, bell pepper, and mushrooms and simmer until carrot is tender but not soft. Add tomatoes, season with salt and black pepper, and simmer, uncovered, for 10 minutes.

Return chicken to the pot and bring sauce to a simmer. Reduce heat to low and cover pot. Cook for 40 minutes; then check the largest piece of chicken for doneness. If it needs to cook longer, stir and cover the pot. Check again after 5 minutes and repeat until chicken is fully cooked. Remove chicken to a platter and continue to simmer the sauce, if necessary, until any wateriness evaporates. To serve, spoon sauce over the chicken.

Roasted Balsamic Chicken

SERVES 4-6

The sweet tanginess of balsamic vinegar intensifies with cooking, making this super-easy dish super-satisfying. You could use boneless parts, but bone-in chicken comes out juicier and more flavorful. This recipe can also be adapted for grilling: Put the chicken over the fire and reduce the marinade in a small saucepan over medium-high heat.

1 (3- to 4-pound) chicken cut up into parts, or an equal weight of precut, bone-in parts

¾ cup balsamic vinegar

3 tablespoons extra-virgin olive oil, plus more for greasing baking dish

3 garlic cloves, chopped

1 tablespoon fresh oregano, chopped

2 tablespoons fresh parsley, chopped

1 teaspoon salt

½ teaspoon freshly ground black pepper

Rinse chicken and pat dry. In a large mixing bowl, whisk together vinegar, oil, garlic, oregano, parsley, salt, and pepper. Add chicken and use your hands to tumble and massage it, coating with the marinade. Refrigerate for at least 30 minutes, tumbling every 10 minutes to marinate.

Preheat the oven to 400°F.

Remove chicken from the refrigerator and grease a 9-×-13-inch baking dish with olive oil. Arrange chicken pieces in the dish and pour marinade over the top. Bake for 20 minutes; then spoon the marinade over the chicken. Bake for another 20 minutes, and check the largest piece of chicken for doneness. If necessary, baste again and bake another 5 minutes. Repeat the process until chicken is done. Let chicken rest for 5 minutes; then plate it and drizzle with pan juices.

Scalloped Chicken or Veal

SERVES 4

In the Francese, Parmigiana, Piccata, and Marsala recipes that follow, chicken or veal work equally well; make your choice based on your own tastes. Thin fillets of chicken or veal are called scallops or, in Italian, scallopine, and they are prepared the same way for each of the recipes. Here how it's done.

If you're making chicken, use skinless, boneless chicken breasts; each breast will yield two cutlets, which equal two servings. Even easier is to buy presliced cutlets in your supermarket. Allow about ¼ pound per serving. If you're making veal, the cutlets will also come presliced for you. Veal cutlets tend to be smaller than chicken cutlets, so you may need more than one per serving. Again, allow about ¼ pound per serving.

....

1 pound boneless, skinless chicken breasts, chicken cutlets, or veal cutlets

½ cup all-purpose flour

1½ teaspoons salt

½ teaspoon freshly ground pepper

3 tablespoons unsalted butter

4 tablespoons olive oil

....

To make chicken cutlets, first rinse meat and pat dry. Cut breasts in half sandwich-wise. Butterfly them open and separate the halves.

To make scallops, place the chicken or veal cutlets between pieces of plastic wrap and gently use a meat hammer or rolling pin to flatten them to ¼-inch thickness.

Combine flour, salt, and pepper on a plate. Dredge each scallop on both sides, shaking off the excess. Place in a single layer on a clean plate and set aside.

Cover a clean plate with a double layer of paper towels. In a large skillet over medium-high heat, melt butter into olive oil until hot but not smoking. Place half of the scallops in the pan in a single layer and brown on both sides, about 1 minute per side. Remove to the paper-towel-covered plate and repeat for the remaining two cutlets. Use these in the recipes that follow.

Chicken or Veal Francese

SERVES 4

Made "in the French manner," according to its Italian name, this preparation is known neither in France nor in Italy. Once again Italian-Americans can take credit for creating this elegant, perfect dish.

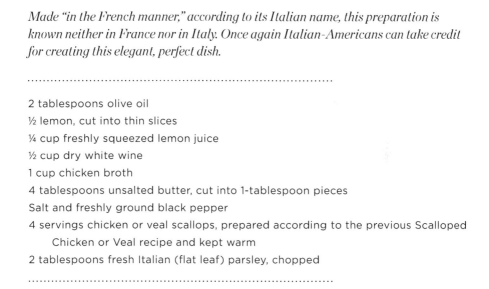

2 tablespoons olive oil

½ lemon, cut into thin slices

¼ cup freshly squeezed lemon juice

½ cup dry white wine

1 cup chicken broth

4 tablespoons unsalted butter, cut into 1-tablespoon pieces

Salt and freshly ground black pepper

4 servings chicken or veal scallops, prepared according to the previous Scalloped Chicken or Veal recipe and kept warm

2 tablespoons fresh Italian (flat leaf) parsley, chopped

Add the olive oil to the skillet (uncleaned) that you used to cook the scallopine, and cook lemon slices over medium heat to release their aroma, about 2 minutes. Add lemon juice, wine, and broth, and bring to a vigorous simmer. Cook to reduce the sauce by half, about 5 minutes. Melt in butter, season with salt and pepper, and whisk sauce for 30 seconds. Reduce heat to medium-low.

Return scallopine to the pan and simmer to heat through, about 2 minutes. Plate immediately with lemon slices on top, spooning sauce over the scallopine. Garnish with parsley.

Chicken or Veal Parmigiana

SERVES 4

Nothing could be simpler than this indulgent dish, a star on pizzeria and mom-and-pop menus across America. On a crusty, soft roll, it makes a fantastic sandwich.

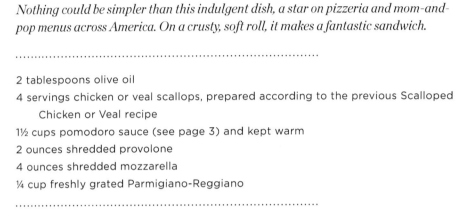

2 tablespoons olive oil

4 servings chicken or veal scallops, prepared according to the previous Scalloped Chicken or Veal recipe

1½ cups pomodoro sauce (see page 3) and kept warm

2 ounces shredded provolone

4 ounces shredded mozzarella

¼ cup freshly grated Parmigiano-Reggiano

Move the broiler pan to the second-lowest rung. Preheat broiler to high.

Grease bottom and sides of a 9-×-9-inch baking dish with olive oil. Lay the scallopine in the dish and spread the pomodoro sauce over the scallopine. Sprinkle on the provolone, mozzarella, and Parmigiano-Reggiano.

Place dish in the oven (not the broiler) for 1 minute; then move it under the broiler and cook until cheese melts, about 2 minutes.

Chicken or Veal Piccata

SERVES 4

Zesty and piquant, this lemony dish wakes up white meat, whether you choose to make it with chicken breasts or veal cutlets. Use up to ⅓ cup of lemon juice if you like a little extra zing on your plate.

1 cup white wine
¼ cup fresh lemon juice
½ cup chicken stock
1 garlic clove, chopped
3 tablespoons capers
3 tablespoons unsalted butter
2 tablespoons fresh parsley, chopped
Salt and freshly ground black pepper
4 servings chicken or veal scallops, prepared according to the previous Scalloped Chicken or Veal recipe and kept warm

In the skillet (uncleaned) used to cook the scallopine, bring wine to a boil over medium heat and deglaze, scraping all brown bits off the bottom. Reduce wine by half and add lemon juice, stock, garlic, and capers. Reduce heat to medium and cook liquid until slightly thickened, about 5 minutes.

Whisk in butter until it melts; then stir in parsley. Season with salt and pepper.

Return scallopine to pan and cook for 1 to 2 minutes, until sauce thickens and meat heats through. Plate immediately, spooning sauce over the scallopine.

Chicken or Veal Scallopine with Marsala Sauce

SERVES 4

The key to this recipe is to use dry, rather than sweet, Marsala, which is a fortified wine that has a higher alcohol content than regular wine, as a preservative. Marsala comes in both dry and sweet varieties; if you can't find the dry version, you can substitute dry Madeira or dry sherry. Any of these fortified wines will keep for a long time in your pantry, so you can use them for other sauces and gravies.

¾ cup dry Marsala

½ pound white or cremini mushrooms, de-stemmed and caps cut into thin slices

1 cup chicken broth

3 tablespoons unsalted butter

Sea salt and freshly ground black pepper

4 servings chicken or veal scallops, prepared according to the previous Scalloped Chicken or Veal recipe kept warm

2 tablespoons fresh Italian (flat leaf) parsley, chopped

To the (uncleaned) skillet used to cook the scallopine, add the Marsala, and deglaze the pan over medium heat, scraping up brown bits from the bottom. Simmer the wine for 1 minute to cook out the alcohol.

Add mushrooms and cook until softened, 4 to 5 minutes. Pour in broth and simmer for 2 minutes to reduce sauce slightly. Swirl in butter and season with salt and pepper.

Return scallopine to the pan, spoon sauce over them, and simmer for 1 minute to heat through. Plate immediately, spooning sauce over the scallopine. Garnish with parsley.

Veal Saltimboca alla Romana

SERVES 4

Once you taste this dish, you'll know why it's called saltimbocca, *literally "jumps in the mouth." It's a classic of the hopping city of Rome.*

....

8 slices prosciutto (about ¼ pound)
8 or more sage leaves (1 or 2 per cutlet, depending on size)
4 servings chicken or veal cutlets, flattened into scallops according to the
     previous Scalloped Chicken or Veal recipe, but not cooked
½ cup all-purpose flour
1½ teaspoons salt
½ teaspoon freshly ground pepper
3 tablespoons unsalted butter, divided
2 tablespoons olive oil
½ cup dry white wine
Salt and freshly ground pepper, to taste
2 tablespoons fresh Italian (flat leaf) parsley, chopped

....

Cut prosciutto into pieces that match the size of the scallops. Lay 1 or 2 pieces of prosciutto and 1 or 2 sage leaves on top of scallops; larger scallops should get more topping than smaller ones. Thread a toothpick through each saltimbocca to secure the prosciutto and sage. Combine flour, salt, and pepper on a plate. Dredge each saltimbocca on both sides, shaking off the excess. Place in a single layer on a clean plate and set aside.

In a large skillet over medium heat, melt 2 tablespoons butter into olive oil until hot but not smoking. Place half of the saltimboccas in a single layer in the pan, prosciutto side down, and cook until prosciutto starts to crisp, about 3 minutes. Turn over and brown the second side, about 2 minutes. Transfer to paper-towel-covered plate and remove toothpicks. Repeat for the remaining saltimboccas.

Raise heat to medium-high, add wine, and bring to a simmer. Deglaze the pan, scraping up brown bits from the bottom. Simmer for at least 1 minute to cook off alcohol. Pour in the broth and add remaining tablespoon of butter, stir to melt the butter, and season with salt and pepper. Plate the saltimboccas, spoon sauce over the top, and garnish with the parsley.

Veal Chops Milanese

SERVES 4

In Milan's kitchens, this dish is usually prepared with bone-in chops, but working with the boneless variety is a lot easier.

....

3 large Roma tomatoes, cored, seeded, and roughly chopped

½ small red onion, sliced into very thin crescents

1 cup torn-up basil leaves

Juice of 1 medium lemon

½ cup extra-virgin olive oil, divided

Sea salt

1 cup all-purpose flour

½ teaspoon freshly ground black pepper

3 eggs, beaten

2 tablespoons fresh Italian (flat-leaf) parsley, chopped

1½ cups fine bread crumbs, made with stale, not toasted, country bread, crusts on

½ cup freshly grated Parmigiano-Reggiano or Pecorino Romano

4 servings veal shoulder chops, flattened using technique from the previous
     Scalloped Chicken or Veal recipe

1 medium lemon, cut into 8 wedges

....

Heat oven to 200°F and place a baking sheet inside.

In a medium mixing bowl, combine tomatoes, onion, and basil and toss with lemon juice and 2 tablespoons oil. Season with salt and set aside.

In a wide, shallow bowl, combine flour with the pepper and 1½ teaspoons salt. In another wide, shallow bowl, combine eggs and the parsley. In a third wide, shallow bowl, combine bread crumbs, cheese, and parsley. Dredge both sides of a veal chop in the flour and shake to remove excess. Dip chop into the egg to coat entirely and let any excess drip off. Lay the chop in the bread-crumb mixture and pat gently to make the crumbs adhere; then turn the chop over and repeat on the other side. Place the chop on a clean plate and lay a piece of waxed paper on top. Repeat with the remaining chops.

In a large skillet over medium-high heat, heat remaining olive oil to hot but not smoking. One at a time, lay each chop in the pan and cook until golden, 2 to 3 minutes per side. As each chop is cooked, place it on the baking sheet in the oven to keep warm. When all chops are cooked, place each on a dinner plate and top with tomato mixture. Serve with lemon wedges on the side.

Polpette in Spicy Tomato Sauce

SERVES 4–6

Like a lot of old red-sauce standbys, spaghetti and meatballs doesn't come from Italy: It was invented right here in the USA by Italian immigrants. Back home, meatballs (polpette) were eaten on their own, as they still are today. But this recipe will do your pasta proud—unless you decide to eat them the Italian way, in a bowl with bread on the side, or in small portions as an antipasto.

3 cups torn-up, crust-off slices of day-old, hearty white bread

1 cup milk

¾ pound sweet Italian sausages

¾ pound ground veal

2 eggs, beaten

3 tablespoons freshly grated Parmigiano-Reggiano

2 tablespoons fresh oregano, chopped

¼ cup fresh Italian (flat leaf) parsley, finely chopped

¾ teaspoon salt

½ teaspoon freshly ground black pepper

¾ cup olive oil

6 cups marinara sauce (see page 2)

Freshly grated Parmigiano-Reggiano or Pecorino Romano, for sprinkling on top

In a small mixing bowl, soak bread in the milk. While it soaks, slit the sausages open lengthwise and remove stuffing from casings. Discard casings and put sausage meat into a large mixing bowl. Remove bread from the milk and tear into smaller pieces. Add to the large bowl along with veal, eggs, cheese, oregano, parsley, salt, and pepper. Use your hands to combine ingredients well. Wash your hands and keep them moist.

Remove a portion of the meat mixture from the bowl, and roll between your palms to form a ball about the size of a golf ball. Set the meatball on waxed paper. Repeat until all of the meat mixture is used up.

In a large skillet over medium heat, heat oil until it is hot but not smoking. Into the pan put as many meatballs as will fit without crowding and that can be turned to brown on all sides. Cook, turning occasionally, until golden brown all over, about 10 minutes. If cooking in batches, remove the cooked meatballs before adding uncooked meatballs to the pan. Put the cooked meatballs in a large saucepan.

When all meatballs are ready, place the saucepan on the stove over medium heat. Add the marinara sauce and bring to a boil; then lower heat to medium-low. Simmer for 25 minutes. To plate, put the meatballs in bowls and spoon some sauce over the top. Serve with grated cheese for sprinkling on top and crusty bread on the side. Reserve any extra sauce for another use.

Pork Chops Porchetta Style

SERVES 4

Here's an easy way to enjoy the flavors of porchetta (pronounced "porketta"), a Roman pork roast that's often eaten in sandwiches. The traditional preparation is a rolled roast of pork loin and pork belly with fennel and herbs; this quick recipe instead stuffs pork chops with porchetta's distinctive layers of flavor.

1 small fennel bulb with fronds

3 tablespoons olive oil, divided

2 garlic cloves, sliced very thin

2 tablespoons fresh rosemary, finely chopped

2 tablespoons fresh sage, finely chopped

1 tablespoon fresh thyme, finely chopped

2 teaspoons fennel seeds

Salt

4 thick, bone-in pork chops

Freshly ground black pepper

¾ cup dry white wine

2 tablespoons butter

Preheat the oven to 350°F.

Cut the green, feathery fronds off the fennel, chop, and reserve for garnish. Cut the fennel bulb in half and slice into thin crescents. In a large skillet heat 2 tablespoons oil over medium heat until hot but not smoking. Add fennel bulb and garlic, and sauté until softened and lightly browned, about 10 minutes. Add rosemary, sage, thyme, fennel seeds, and ½ teaspoon salt, and cook, stirring constantly, for about 5 minutes. Transfer the fennel mixture to a bowl, and set it aside to cool. Reserve pan with the remnants.

Rinse the chops and pat dry. Lay on a work surface and, holding each down with the palm of your hand, slice horizontally into the fatty edge to cut a deep pocket in the meat. Sprinkle chops inside and out with salt and black pepper. Stuff pockets with the fennel mixture, reserving any excess filling.

Place the skillet used to cook fennel mixture over high heat, and add the remaining tablespoon of oil. Lay the chops in the pan and cook until golden brown on one side, about 3 minutes. Turn them over and brown on the other side, about 3 minutes. Transfer chops to a baking dish and coat with any reserved filling. Cook in the oven until done but still moist, 5 to 10 minutes depending on size. Remove dish from the oven, and let the chops rest for 10 minutes.

While the meat is resting, return skillet to the stove over medium heat. Add wine and deglaze, scraping brown bits off of the bottom of the pan. Reduce the wine by one third and whisk in butter. Place each chop on a dinner plate, spoon over some sauce, and garnish with reserved fennel fronds.

Roasted Pork Tenderloin with Porcini

SERVES 4–6

Italian cooks revere the wild forest mushroom called porcini, and put it in everything from risotto to pasta to soup. Fresh porcini are available only in late summer and autumn, but during the rest of the year—and all year outside Europe—dried porcini are the rule. And a lovely rule it is.

....

1½ ounces dried porcini

2 pounds pork tenderloin

Sea salt

2 tablespoons olive oil

2 teaspoons fresh rosemary, minced

3 garlic cloves, minced

2 shallots, minced

½ cup dry Marsala or Madeira (see note in the Chicken or Veal Scallopine with Marsala Sauce recipe, earlier)

½ cup dry white wine

1 cup low-salt chicken broth

1 tablespoon butter, softened

1 tablespoon all-purpose flour

....

Preheat the oven to 400°F.

In a small bowl, soak mushrooms in warm water for 30 minutes.

Sprinkle pork all over with salt. In a large skillet heat oil over medium-high, add rosemary and garlic, and cook for 30 seconds. Increase heat to high and place pork in the pan. Brown pork evenly on all sides, about 5 minutes; then transfer to a baking dish. Leave rosemary in the pan. Cook pork in the oven until it is done but still moist, 15 to 20 minutes. Remove dish from the oven and allow the pork to rest while you make the sauce.

While the pork is roasting, pour mushrooms into a strainer above a small bowl and reserve the liquid. Finely chop mushrooms and set aside. Reheat skillet over medium; then add shallots to the rosemary and garlic, and sauté until tender, about 5 minutes. Add Marsala and white wine, increase heat to high, and boil the liquid until most of it evaporates, about 7 minutes. Add chopped mushrooms, mushroom liquid, and broth, and bring sauce back to a boil. Cook until sauce is reduced to about 1½ cups, about 15 minutes; then reduce heat to medium-low. In a small bowl, blend together butter and flour and whisk the paste into the sauce. Simmer to slightly thicken the sauce, about 2 minutes, and season with salt and pepper.

To serve, cut the tenderloin into ¼-inch-thick slices and top with sauce.

Beef Braciole

SERVES 4-6

A Sunday dinner favorite in many Italian-American homes, beef braciole are made by rolling up thin slices of steak with a filling of bread crumbs seasoned with a variety of delectable additions. The rolls are also known as involtini.

....

1½ cups plain bread crumbs

2 tablespoons butter, melted

3 garlic cloves, minced

½ cup freshly grated Parmigiano-Reggiano or Pecorino Romano

½ cup fresh Italian (flat-leaf) parsley, chopped

1 tablespoon fresh oregano, chopped

Salt and freshly ground black pepper

1 (1½-pound) thin flank steak

¼ pound prosciutto, thinly sliced

¼ cup olive oil

¼ cup dry red wine

3½ cups Pomodoro Sauce (see page 3)

....

Put bread crumbs in a medium mixing bowl and stir in butter. Add garlic, cheese, parsley, oregano, ½ teaspoon salt, and ⅛ teaspoon pepper and mix well. Set aside.

Place steak in the middle of a large, flat work surface. Cutting across the grain of the meat every 2 inches or so, score it with parallel slices about ¼ inch deep. Cover the meat with a piece of wax paper or plastic wrap about twice the size of the meat. With a meat hammer or rolling pin, flatten the steak to about ¼ to ½ inch thick. Peel off the wrapping.

Sprinkle steak with salt and pepper. Lay the slices of prosciutto over steak to cover its entire surface. Spoon the bread crumb mixture onto the meat and spread out evenly, leaving a ¼-inch border uncovered around the edges. Starting from the longest edge, roll the meat like a jelly roll. With the seam edge down, slice the roll into 4 to 6 pieces—no piece should be more than 4 inches long. Use cotton string to tie the rolls closed on each end.

In a large skillet heat oil over medium-high until it is hot but not smoking. Place rolls in the pan so they don't touch, and brown them all around, a total of 5 or 6 minutes. It may be necessary to do this in batches to allow enough room in the pan. Set the browned rolls aside on a plate.

Reduce heat to medium and pour in wine. Bring wine to a boil and deglaze pan, scraping brown bits off the bottom. Add the pomodoro sauce and bring to a simmer. Return rolls to the pan, reduce heat to medium-low, and partially cover. Simmer gently for 1 hour, stirring occasionally. Transfer rolls to a serving platter, snip off strings, and cut rolls into 1-inch-thick slices. Spoon sauce over the top and serve.

Beef Braised in Red Wine

SERVES 6

Leave it to the Italians to elevate the humble pot roast to such culinary heights. The key to this dish is the wine: Beef should be braised in a big, bold red wine—the same kind of wine you might drink with your meal. Most traditional is the Piedmontese wine Barolo, but other reds from that region(i.e., Barbaresco and Barbera) are good options, too. If you can't find any of these, try Shiraz, Zinfandel, or California Syrah.

....

5 tablespoons unsalted butter, divided

1 (4-pound) boneless beef chuck roast or rump roast

1 small onion, finely chopped

2 garlic cloves, halved

1 celery stalk, diced

1 medium carrot, diced

½ teaspoon fresh thyme, chopped

1 dried bay leaf

1 teaspoon salt

½ teaspoon freshly ground black pepper

1 bottle (3 cups) dry red wine

....

Preheat the oven to 350°F.

In a large skillet over medium-high heat, melt 3 tablespoons butter until it bubbles. Put roast in the pan and brown on every side, 10 to 15 minutes. Set aside.

Select a saucepan or Dutch oven that has a tight-fitting lid and is large enough to hold the roast when covered. Over medium heat, melt the remaining 2 tablespoons butter and cook the onion until lightly browned. Add garlic, celery, carrot, thyme, bay leaf, salt, and pepper; stir well; and cook for 5 minutes.

Transfer roast to the pot. With 1 cup of wine, deglaze the browning skillet, scraping brown bits off the bottom. Add liquid to the pot with the roast. Pour remaining wine into the pot, and add water if needed to cover the roast two-thirds of the way with liquid. Increase heat to high and bring liquid to a boil, stirring well. Cover pot and put it in the oven for about 3 hours, turning and basting every 30 minutes. If the pot dries out while cooking, add another ¼ cup water.

When roast is done, move pot from oven to stove top. Transfer the roast to a cutting board and cover with aluminum foil to sit for 10 minutes. Remove bay leaf from the pot. If pan juices are still thin, increase heat to high and reduce while scraping any brown bits off bottom and sides of pot.

To serve, slice roast and spoon pan juices over the top.

Grilled Steak Tagliata

SERVES 4-6

In your lifetime, you've probably grilled a thousand steaks. What more could you possibly need to know? Well, this is how it's done in northern Italy. The secret is in the simplicity and the serving. Tagliata *means "sliced," and that's just how this steak comes to the table, its rare (Italians like their steaks* RARE*) saltiness perfectly offset by the fresh bitterness of arugula and the tangy acidity of lemon. If you can't grill, try searing the steak in a cast-iron pan and finishing it in the oven.*

⋯⋯⋯⋯⋯⋯⋯⋯⋯⋯⋯⋯⋯⋯⋯⋯⋯⋯⋯⋯⋯⋯⋯⋯⋯⋯⋯⋯⋯⋯⋯⋯

½ cup extra-virgin olive oil, plus more for brushing and drizzling

½ cup balsamic vinegar

2 tablespoons fresh rosemary, chopped

3 garlic cloves, minced

Sea salt and freshly ground black pepper

One 2-pound flank steak (or substitute strip or sirloin)

½ pound arugula

1 lemon, cut into wedges

2-ounce chunk Parmigiano-Reggiano

⋯⋯⋯⋯⋯⋯⋯⋯⋯⋯⋯⋯⋯⋯⋯⋯⋯⋯⋯⋯⋯⋯⋯⋯⋯⋯⋯⋯⋯⋯⋯⋯

In a medium mixing bowl, whisk together oil, vinegar, rosemary, garlic, 1 teaspoon salt, and ½ teaspoon pepper. Pour marinade into a baking dish large enough to hold the steak. Add steak and turn over a few times to coat with the marinade. Cover tightly with plastic wrap and refrigerate for at least 1 hour.

Take steak out of refrigerator and allow it to come to room temperature. Preheat grill or cast-iron pan to high. Remove meat from the marinade and sprinkle all over with salt and pepper; discard the marinade. Brush grill rack or pan with oil. Put the steak on the heat and cook until it has a deep brown crust on both sides, 4 minutes per side for rare or 5 to 6 minutes per side for medium rare. The meat will get tough if cooked longer. Transfer the steak to a cutting board and allow it to rest for 5 minutes.

On a large serving platter, spread out a bed of arugula and drizzle lightly with olive oil. Place the lemon wedges around the edge of the platter. Slice the steak against the grain, on the diagonal, into pieces ½ inch thick or thinner. Arrange slices in the middle of arugula bed. Use a cheese plane or vegetable peeler to shave the cheese over the platter.

Lamb Chops Scottadito

SERVES 4-6

In Rome it's traditional to eat these grilled lamb chops with one's hands when they're sizzling-hot off the grill: That's why they're called scottadito, or "burning fingers." Cook them either on the grill or in the broiler.

½ cup extra-virgin olive oil

3 garlic cloves, sliced thin

2 tablespoons fresh rosemary, chopped

Salt and freshly ground black pepper

12 rib lamb chops, 1¼ inches thick (about 3 pounds total)

1 large lemon, cut into wedges

In a small mixing bowl, combine oil, garlic, rosemary, 1 teaspoon salt, and ½ teaspoon pepper. Put chops in a baking dish and pour in marinade. Turn and massage the chops to coat on all sides. Cover tightly with plastic wrap and refrigerate for about 2 hours.

Take chops out of refrigerator and allow them to come to room temperature. Preheat grill or broiler to high. Grill or broil chops until well browned on the outside and pink on the inside, about 4 minutes per side. Transfer chops to a warm platter and serve hot, with lemon wedges on the side.

CHAPTER NINE

Desserts

If Americans agree that you can never be too rich or too thin, Italians agree that desserts should never be too rich or too sweet. An ordinary meal on an ordinary day wraps up with a little cheese, some fresh fruit, or a small bite of chocolate, accompanied by a shot of espresso or a glass of wine.

That being said, some of the world's greatest and most decadent desserts come from Italy. Think of masterpieces like gelato, cannoli, and tiramisu. Then there are hundreds of varieties of mouthwatering cookies, custards, cakes, candies, and frozen treats. And let's not forget those spectacular, sumptuous pastries that are as breathtaking to gaze upon as they are to eat. Even the tiniest village seems to have a *pasticceria* (pastry shop) and a *gelateria,* and in big cities some streets and squares are lined with shop windows displaying row upon row of colorful, irresistible sweets.

Some of the desserts Italians eat today go back thousands of years. Italian ice supposedly dates back to ancient Roman times, as does the nougat candy *torrone.* The Romans are also credited with inventing custard. Dessert was high fashion in Renaissance Florence, where Catherine de Medici popularized sorbet and Maria de Medici got married to . . . a life-size sugar sculpture of her groom, King Henry IV of France (he couldn't make it to the wedding). Down through the centuries, new desserts have been created to celebrate Italian holidays, historic events, and special occasions. Many of them are so special they are eaten only once a year.

Chocolate, cream, butter, flour, and, of course, sugar are cornerstones of Italian confectionery, but some of its other signature ingredients give it a distinct accent. Nuts, especially almonds and hazelnuts, as well as pignoli and chestnuts, feature prominently, as do dried and candied fruits such as currants and orange and lemon peel. Liquor and wine are frequently incorporated as well. Also in the mix are some ingredients that you might not consider when you think of dessert, such as olive oil, polenta, ricotta, and semolina. Combine all these scrumptious elements in a bowl, and you've got a sweet ending to your Italian-style meal. After all, Italians love *la dolce vita*—the sweet life.

Affogato

SERVES 2

In Italian, the word affogato *means "drowned," and that's just what happens to the ice cream in this ever-so-easy dessert. The marriage of sugar and coffee is bound to perk you up after a filling meal.*

....

1 cup vanilla, chocolate, or coffee ice cream
2 (2-ounce) shots espresso or 6 tablespoons very strong brewed coffee, hot
½ cup whipped cream (optional)

....

Scoop ½ cup ice cream into each of 2 coffee cups. Pour 1 shot espresso or 3 tablespoons brewed coffee over ice cream. Top with whipped cream (if using).

Lemon-Ricotta Cookies

MAKES 3–4 DOZEN COOKIES

Italian cookies tend to be drier and more crumbly than cookies made in the USA, but these are soft and moist. That's the ricotta at work.

....

To make the cookies:

2¼ cups all-purpose flour

1 teaspoon baking powder

1 teaspoon salt

1 stick (½ cup) unsalted butter, softened

1 cup sugar

2 eggs

1 (15-ounce) container ricotta cheese, drained

½ teaspoon vanilla extract

3 tablespoons lemon juice

Zest of 1 lemon

....

Move oven racks to middle and top rungs, and preheat the oven to 350°F. Line two baking sheets with parchment paper or silicone baking mats. Sift together flour, baking powder, and salt into a medium mixing bowl. Set aside.

In a large bowl, use an electric mixer on high speed to cream butter with the sugar until light and fluffy, 2 to 3 minutes. Switch to medium speed and add eggs one at a time, beating each until thoroughly combined with the butter. Add ricotta, vanilla, lemon juice, and lemon zest, and continue to beat to incorporate. Reduce to low speed and add dry ingredients. Beat just until the ingredients marry.

Scoop heaping tablespoons of the dough onto the baking sheets, 2 inches apart. Slide pans into the oven and bake, switching the pans halfway through the cooking time. The cookies should puff up and turn golden around the edges after 15 to 20 minutes. Remove from the oven and set the cookies in a single layer on wire racks to cool.

To make the glaze:
1½ cups confectioners' sugar, sifted
¼ cup lemon juice, freshly squeezed

While the cookies are cooling, stir together confectioners' sugar and lemon juice in a small mixing bowl until smooth. If the glaze is too thick to spread evenly, add a little water; if it is too thin to stay in place on top of the cookies, add a little sugar.

When the cookies have cooled completely, use a butter spreader to smear glaze over the top of each cookie. Return cookies to wire racks in a single layer, and let the glaze dry for about 2 hours. Store in an airtight container.

Pignoli Cookies

MAKES 2½ DOZEN COOKIES

Pignoli (pine nuts) and almond paste, the two main ingredients of these flourless macaroons, are classic baking ingredients in Italy. Created in Sicily and popular all over the southern part of the country, they're a traditional treat at Christmastime. For this recipe, it's important that you use almond paste, not marzipan.

....

12 ounces (1¼ cups) almond paste
½ cup granulated sugar
¾ cup confectioners' sugar, plus more for dusting
2 egg whites, beaten
1½ cups pignoli

....

Move oven racks to middle and top rungs, and preheat the oven to 325°F. Line two baking sheets with parchment paper or silicone baking mats.

In a small mixing bowl, mash almond paste with granulated sugar to make a crumbly blend. Add confectioners' sugar and combine thoroughly. Add egg whites and mix just until dough comes together.

Put pignoli in a shallow bowl. Dampen your hands and remove about 4 teaspoons of the dough from the mixing bowl. Roll into a ball about 1 inch in diameter, put it into the bowl with the pignoli, and roll around to coat with the nuts. Place the ball onto the baking sheet and press down slightly with your fingers. Repeat until all dough is used, placing the cookies about 2 inches apart.

Slide pans into the oven and bake, switching pans halfway through the cooking time. The cookies should turn pale gold after 15 to 20 minutes; don't allow the nuts to brown. Remove cookies from the oven, let them sit in the pan for 1 minute, and then lay on wire racks to cool. Dust with confectioners' sugar and store in an airtight container.

Almond Biscotti

MAKES 2 DOZEN BISCOTTI

What Americans call biscotti the Italians call cantucci *(biscotti is in fact the Italian word for "cookies" in general). They're baked twice to give them their dry, hard texture, which makes them perfect for dunking. The Italians like to dunk theirs in wine, but you might prefer coffee.*

1½ cups blanched whole almonds
2½ cups all-purpose flour, plus more for work surface
½ teaspoon salt
1 teaspoon baking powder
1 cup granulated sugar
3 eggs
1½ teaspoons almond extract

Move oven racks to the middle and top rungs, and preheat the oven to 350°F.

Spread almonds in a single layer on a baking sheet, and toast on the middle rack of the oven until golden, 8 to 10 minutes. Let them cool in the pan; then chop coarsely and set aside.

Line two baking sheets with parchment paper or silicone baking mats.

Sift together flour, salt, and baking powder into a medium mixing bowl and set aside.

In a large mixing bowl, use an electric mixer on high speed to beat sugar and eggs until thick and creamy, about 5 minutes. Blend in almond extract. Add dry ingredients and mix until well incorporated into wet ingredients. Fold in almonds. On a generously floured work surface, divide dough in half, and roll each half into a log about 12 inches long and 3 inches in diameter. Place the logs on a baking sheet about 5 inches apart, and press down a little with your hands to flatten slightly. Bake until they are golden and firm, 30 to 35 minutes. Remove logs from the oven, and let them cool on a wire rack until you can handle them, about 10 minutes.

Reduce oven temperature to 325°F.

continued ▶

Transfer logs to a cutting board, and use a serrated knife to cut diagonally into ¾-inch-thick slices. Lay the biscotti flat on the baking sheets, 2 inches apart. Slide pans into the oven, and bake until biscotti are golden, about 10 minutes. Remove pans from the oven, flip the biscotti over, and return pans to the oven, switching their positions on racks. Bake until second side is golden, about 10 minutes. Remove pans from oven and let biscotti cool for 5 minutes; then transfer to wire racks to cool completely and harden. Store in an airtight container.

Chocolate Biscotti

MAKES 3 DOZEN BISCOTTI

For a chocolate experience that won't hit you over the head with gooey sweetness, these biscotti fit the bill. If you are allergic to nuts, you can simply leave them out.

....

1 cup blanched hazelnuts

2½ cups flour, plus more for work surface

¾ cups unsweetened cocoa powder

1 tablespoon instant espresso powder

¼ teaspoon salt

1 teaspoon baking soda

¾ teaspoon baking powder

1¼ cups sugar

3 eggs, beaten, with 2 tablespoons reserved

1 teaspoon vanilla extract

....

Move oven racks to middle and top rungs. Preheat the oven to 350°F.

Spread hazelnuts in a single layer on a baking sheet, and toast on the middle rack of the oven until golden, 8 to 10 minutes. Let cool in the pan, then chop coarsely and set aside.

Line two baking sheets with parchment paper or silicone baking mats.

Sift together flour, cocoa powder, espresso powder, salt, baking soda, and baking powder into a medium mixing bowl and set aside.

In a large mixing bowl, use an electric mixer on high speed to beat sugar and eggs until thick and creamy, about 5 minutes. Blend in vanilla extract. Add dry ingredients and mix until well incorporated into wet ingredients. Fold in hazelnuts.

On a generously floured work surface, divide dough in half and roll each half into a log about 12 inches long and 3 inches in diameter. Place logs on a baking sheet about 5 inches apart, and press down a little with your hands to flatten slightly. Brush tops with the reserved egg, and bake until firm, 25 to 30 minutes. Remove logs from the oven and let cool on a wire rack until you can handle them, about 5 minutes.

continued ▶

Reduce oven temperature to 325°F.

Transfer logs to a cutting board and use a serrated knife to cut diagonally into ¾-inch-thick slices. Lay biscotti flat on the baking sheets, 2 inches apart. Slide pans into the oven and bake until biscotti are dry on one side, about 10 minutes. Remove pans from oven, flip biscotti over, and return pans to the oven, switching their positions on racks. Bake until second side is dry, about 10 minutes. Remove pans from the oven and let biscotti cool for 5 minutes; then transfer to wire racks to cool completely and harden. Store in an airtight container.

Flourless Chocolate Cake

MAKES 1 (9-INCH) TORTA

By all accounts, torta caprese, *the best-known Italian version of flourless chocolate cake, originated by accident on the island of Capri. No one knows exactly how it happened: There are tales of bakers who mistook cocoa powder or ground almonds for flour, and of cooks simply forgetting to add flour. Whatever went down, the result is a chocoholic's dream. Gelato, ice cream, and whipped cream make great toppings.*

....

1¾ cups blanched almonds
¼ cup unsweetened cocoa powder
1 tablespoon vanilla extract
1 cup granulated sugar
5 eggs, room temperature
8 ounces high-quality dark chocolate (not unsweetened), chopped into
    small pieces
1 cup (2 sticks) unsalted butter
Confectioners' sugar for dusting

....

Preheat the oven to 350° F. Line the bottom of a 9-inch regular or spring-form cake pan with a round of parchment paper or wax paper.

Spread the almonds in a single layer on a baking sheet, and toast on the middle rack of oven until golden, 8 to 10 minutes. Let cool in the pan, then grind in a food processor or coffee grinder and set aside. You should end up with 1¼ to 1½ cups.

In a large mixing bowl, combine cocoa powder, vanilla, and sugar. Beat in eggs one at a time, mixing thoroughly, and set aside.

Melt chocolate and butter in a double boiler, or in a metal or glass bowl fit snugly on top of a medium saucepan: Fill the saucepan or the bottom of the double boiler with 2 or 3 inches of water. The water should not touch the upper container. Set the lower pot over low heat, and bring the water to a low simmer; then turn off heat, place the upper container on top, and put in the chocolate. When the chocolate starts to melt, begin stirring gently and steadily. Let almost all of the

continued ▶

chocolate melt; then remove the upper container from its place on the stove to the counter. Continue stirring until chocolate and butter are completely melted into a satiny cream.

Whisk melted chocolate into the cocoa-egg mixture, and then add almonds. Pour the batter into the pan, spread it evenly, and smooth it out on top. Bake until the cake starts separating from the side of the pan and a knife inserted in the center comes out with only a few moist crumbs, about 50 minutes. Set the pan on a wire rack, and let the cake cool for 5 minutes; then invert the pan onto another rack to release the cake. Peel off the parchment or wax paper and discard. When the cake has cooled completely, invert onto a serving plate and dust with confectioners' sugar.

Olive Oil Cake

MAKES 1 (10-INCH) CAKE

Yup, olive oil. There's no butter or shortening in this recipe, only a little of Italy's liquid gold. The olive oil makes this cake especially moist and tender, and lends a savory hint to the lightly sweet flavor. Use a milder extra-virgin olive oil rather than one of the peppery ones, and don't substitute vegetable or other oils the results will be inferior.

....

¾ cup extra-virgin olive oil, plus more for greasing the pan

1½ cups all-purpose flour

1½ teaspoons baking powder

1 teaspoon salt

3 eggs

¾ cup granulated sugar

⅓ cup freshly squeezed orange juice

Zest of ½ medium orange

½ cup milk

Confectioners' sugar, for dusting

....

Move oven rack to upper portion of the oven, and preheat to 350° F. Grease the bottom and sides of a 9-inch regular or spring-form cake pan with olive oil.

In a small mixing bowl, combine flour, baking powder, and salt. Set aside.

In a large mixing bowl, beat eggs briefly and add sugar. Beat eggs and sugar until foamy, about 30 seconds. Add olive oil, orange juice, and orange zest; combine thoroughly, and then beat in milk. Add dry ingredients and continue beating until everything is well combined and batter is smooth.

Pour batter into the pan and bake until cake starts to pull away from sides of the pan and a knife inserted into the center comes out clean, about 45 minutes. Place the cake on a rack to cool for 10 minutes; then invert it onto a rack to cool completely. Dust with confectioners' sugar.

Ricotta Cheesecake

MAKES 1 (8-INCH) CAKE

This cheesecake has the slightly grainy texture of ricotta and is lighter than conventional American cheesecakes. Top it with chocolate sauce for added flair.

8 ounces biscotti, flavor of your choice

2 tablespoons butter, softened

6 eggs

¾ cup granulated sugar

¼ teaspoon salt

2 (15-ounce) containers ricotta, drained, room temperature

8 ounces mascarpone cheese or cream cheese, room temperature

2 teaspoons vanilla extract

Zest of 1 lemon

Strawberries, raspberries, or blueberries (optional)

Set a rack in center of the oven and preheat to 350°F.

In a food processor, grind biscotti to a fine texture and set aside.

Spread butter on bottom and sides of an 8-inch spring-form cake pan. Put biscotti crumbs in the pan and tilt pan around to coat the inside. Tip out excess crumbs and discard.

In a large mixing bowl, use an electric mixer at high speed to whip together eggs, sugar, and salt for 2 minutes. Beat in ricotta, mascarpone, vanilla, and lemon zest.

Pour batter into the pan, spread it out with a spatula so the top is even and smooth, and place in the oven. Bake the cake until it puffs up and turns light golden around the edges, about 1 hour and 15 minutes. The center should still move when you shake the pan. Set pan on a wire rack to cool completely; the center will sink slightly.

Serve with strawberries, raspberries, or blueberries according to preference.

Milk Chocolate Panna Cotta

SERVES 6

Panna cotta *is Italian for "cooked cream," and this dessert is as silky and rich as it sounds. Top it simply with whipped cream, or try finishing it with caramel sauce or berries.*

Canola oil for greasing the cups
1 cup milk
1 package (2¼ teaspoons) unflavored gelatin
2 cups heavy cream
½ cup sugar
8 ounces high-quality milk chocolate, finely chopped
1 teaspoon vanilla extract
Whipped cream (optional)

Lightly coat bottoms and sides of 6 (6-ounce) custard cups or ramekins with canola oil. Place on a baking sheet and set aside.

Pour milk into a medium mixing bowl, and sprinkle gelatin evenly over the surface. Set aside while gelatin softens, about 5 minutes.

In a medium saucepan over medium-high heat, combine heavy cream and sugar. Stirring to dissolve the sugar, bring cream to a boil. Remove the pot from heat, and stir in chocolate until it melts and combines with the cream. Add vanilla. Pour chocolate mixture into the bowl with the gelatin mixture and whisk to combine.

Remove any undissolved material by pouring the liquid through a sieve into a large measuring cup or other spouted container. Pour liquid evenly into cups, and place baking sheet on a level surface in the refrigerator. Chill until set, about 6 hours. Serve topped with whipped cream, if using.

Tiramisu

SERVES 12

Tales of the origin of tiramisu, literally "pick me up," date it anywhere between the early eighteenth and the late twentieth century. It may have been created in the city of Siena to celebrate a visit by the Grand Duke of Tuscany Cosimo III, or it may have started out as a pick-me-up for hardworking prostitutes in the city of Treviso. Though providing a less colorful story, some food historians believe that tiramisu may simply have originated in an Italian chef's kitchen in 1971.

....

6 egg yolks

¼ cup sugar

1 pound mascarpone cheese (2½ cups), room temperature

1 cup heavy cream

1½ cups espresso or very strong brewed coffee, cool

¼ cup coffee liqueur such as Kahlúa

36 packaged ladyfingers

Unsweetened cocoa powder, for dusting

1 ounce bittersweet chocolate, shaved

....

In a large mixing bowl, beat together egg yolks and sugar with a whisk or electric mixer until mixture is thick and light yellow, about 5 minutes. Then thoroughly beat in mascarpone cheese.

In a medium mixing bowl, whip cream to stiff peaks. Gently fold whipped cream into the mascarpone mixture until well combined.

In a shallow dish, combine coffee and the liqueur. Quickly dip the ladyfingers into the liquid just until they are moistened—if they soak too long they will fall apart. Line the bottom of a 9-×-13-inch baking dish with a single layer of dipped ladyfingers, covering it completely with about 18 pieces. Using a spatula, spread half the mascarpone mixture over the ladyfingers. Dip more ladyfingers in the coffee mixture, and arrange them on top in a single layer. Spread the rest of the mascarpone over the ladyfingers, and dust the top of the tiramisu with the cocoa powder. Cover with plastic wrap and refrigerate for at least 4 hours.

Take the tiramisu out of the refrigerator 30 minutes before serving. Garnish with chocolate shavings and cut into squares to serve.

Index